Strathroy Ontario in Colour Photos, Saving Our History One Photo at a Time

Photography
by Barbara Raué
©2019

Series Name: Cruising Ontario

Book 236: Strathroy

Cover photo: 129 Albert Street, Page 46

©All the photos in this book have been taken with my cameras. I own the rights to them.

Series Name: Cruising Ontario
Saving Our History One Photo at a Time
in colour photos

Books Available in Alphabetical Order:
Aberfoyle, Acton, Ajax, Alton, Amherstburg, Ancaster, Arthur, Auburn, Aylmer, Ayr, Beaver Valley, Belgrave, Belleville, Bloomingdale, Blyth, Brantford, Brockville, Burford, Burlington, Caledon, Caledonia, Cambridge, Carlow, Chatsworth, Clifford, Collingwood, Conestogo, Delhi, Dorchester to Aylmer, Drayton, Drumbo, Dundas, Dunlop, Eden Mills, Elmira, Elora, Erin, Essex, Fergus, Goderich, Grimsby, Guelph, Hagersville, Hamilton, Hanover, Harriston, Hespeler, Jarvis, Kingston, Kingsville, Kitchener, Lake Superior, Lincoln, Linwood, Listowel, London, Lucknow, Merrickville, Mono, Mount Forest, Mount Pleasant, Neustadt, New Hamburg, Newboro, Newport, Niagara-on-the-Lake, Niagara Falls, North Bay, Oakville, Onondaga, Orangeville, Orillia, Oshawa, Owen Sound, Palmerston, Paris, Pelham, Perth, Peterborough, Petrolia, Pickering, Port Colborne, Port Elgin, Portland, Preston, Rockwood, Sarnia, Sault Ste. Marie, Seaforth, Sheffield, Shelburne, Simcoe, Smiths Falls, Smithville, Southampton, St. Catharines, St. George, St. Jacobs, St. Marys, St. Thomas, Stoney Creek, Stratford, Thamesford, Thunder Bay, Tillsonburg, Toronto, Waterdown, Waterford, Waterloo, Welland, Wellesley, West Flamborough, Westport, Whitby, Windsor, Wingham, Woodstock

Book 204-206: Oshawa
Book 207-209: Niagara Falls
Book 210: North Bay
Book 211: Fort Erie
Book 212-215 Haldimand County

Book 216: Sudbury
Book 217: Parry Sound
Book 218-219: Uxbridge
Book 220: Port Perry

Table of Contents

Kittridge Avenue West	Page 6
Victoria Street	Page 11
Frank Street	Page 13
Front Street West	Page 22
Front Street East	Page 42
Albert Street	Page 42
James Street	Page 50
Caradoc Street	Page 53

Strathroy-Caradoc is located west of the City of London.
    After the War of 1812, the British government encouraged thousands of people from Britain to come to Southwestern Ontario. There were three main reasons for this:
1. The British were afraid that Americans would invade through the Sydenham River area again as they had at Baldoon. If there were settlements in the area, the settlers could warn the British and fight against the Americans.
2. In England, the end of the war meant that many soldiers were out of work. They were starving and homeless. In Ireland, landlords had mismanaged the lands, which led to the Potato Famine. Since potatoes were the main source of income and food, thousands of Irish were starving. In Scotland, landlords chose to graze sheep in the Highlands, and they forced the Scottish Highlanders to leave. In an effort to help these people, the British government began to give away land in Upper Canada.

3. Soldiers of the War of 1812 and the war with France expected land rewards from the King of England; there was no land left in Britain to give them. Land in Upper Canada was given away instead.

Land along the Sydenham River was sparsely settled, the land was fertile and flat which made it easier to clear. The river gave settlers fresh water, and power for their water mills. It could also be used as a highway to move goods to Detroit, where they could be sold. A new road had been built between London and Goderich, which made it easier to get to the Sydenham River by land.

When the government gave away land, there were often conditions the new owner had to live up to, including building roads, mills, and armies, but often, it meant inviting immigrants from Britain to live on their land. For example, a settler might receive 20 000 acres of land, but would be forced to give away 5,000 to other settlers. They would be expected to organize how the immigrants would get to the new settlement, what they would do when they arrived (such as raise sheep, beef or cotton), and help them settle in by building churches and schools. This is how settlements and villages were created along the Sydenham river.

In 1830 James Buchanan, the British Consul at New York City, acquired a tract of 1,200 acres of unsettled land in Adelaide Township. His son, John Stewart, settled there and built a sawmill and gristmill on the Sydenham River. These pioneer industries formed the nucleus of a settlement which was named Strathroy means "Red Valley" in Gaelic, and is named after James Buchanan's birthplace in County Tyrone, Ireland. The construction of a branch line of the Great Western Railway through Strathroy in 1856 stimulated the growth of the community. The line was eventually connected to Michigan at Windsor, providing the farmers of Strathroy with an extra market for their produce.

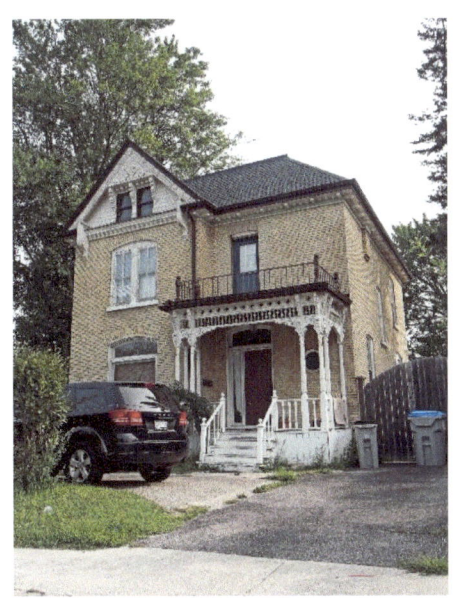

243 – second floor balcony

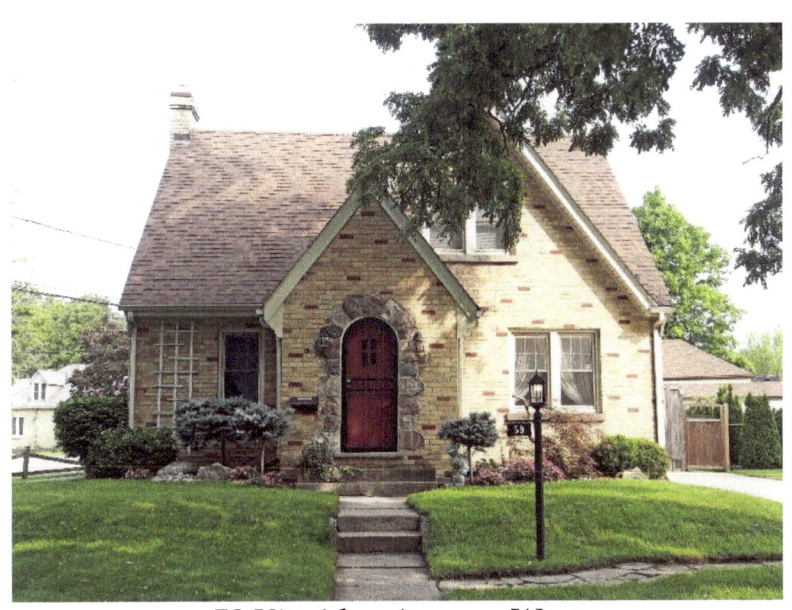

59 Kittridge Avenue West

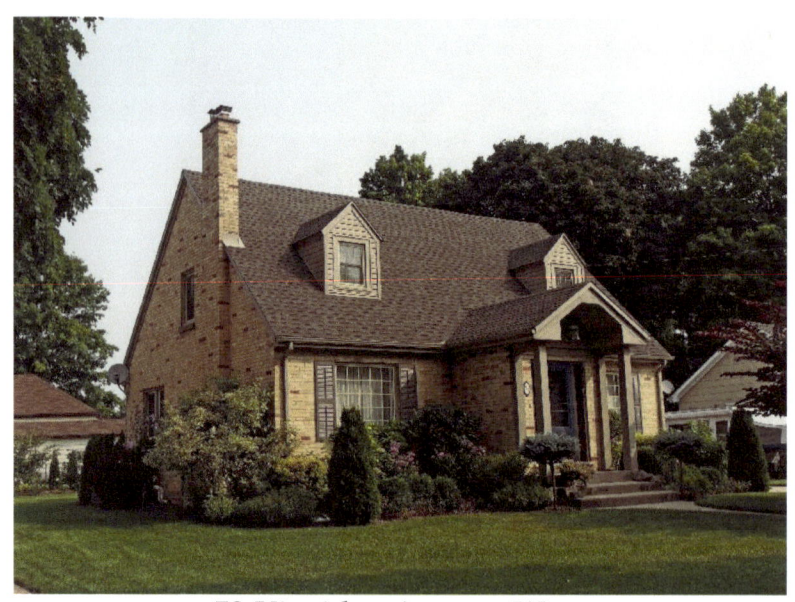

53 Kittridge Avenue West

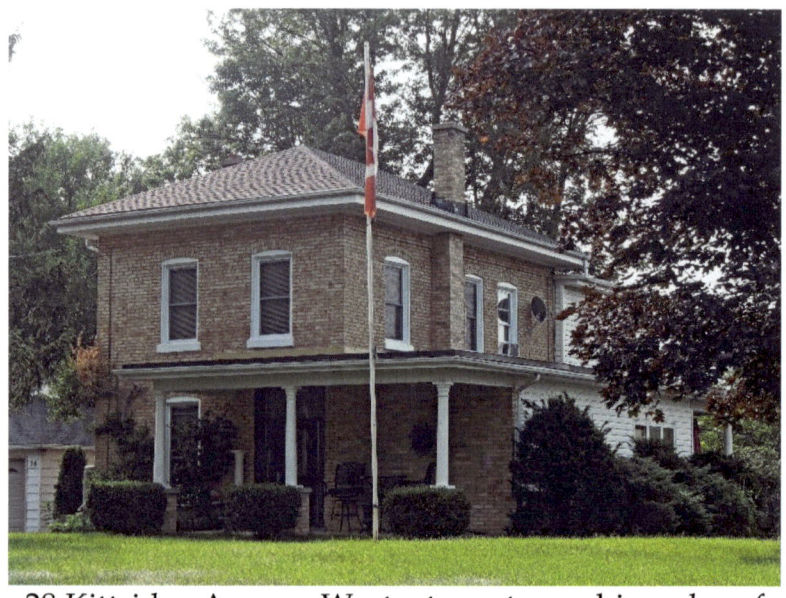

28 Kittridge Avenue West – two-storey, hipped roof

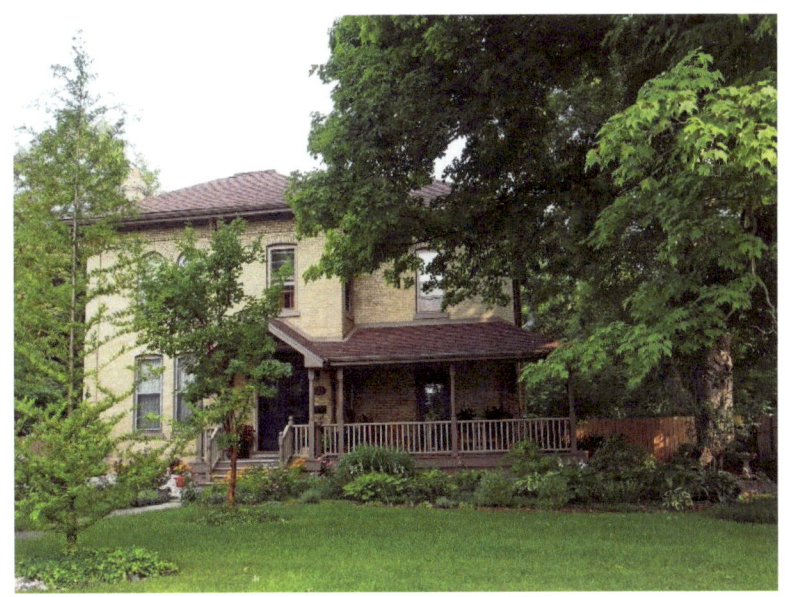

23 Kittridge Avenue West

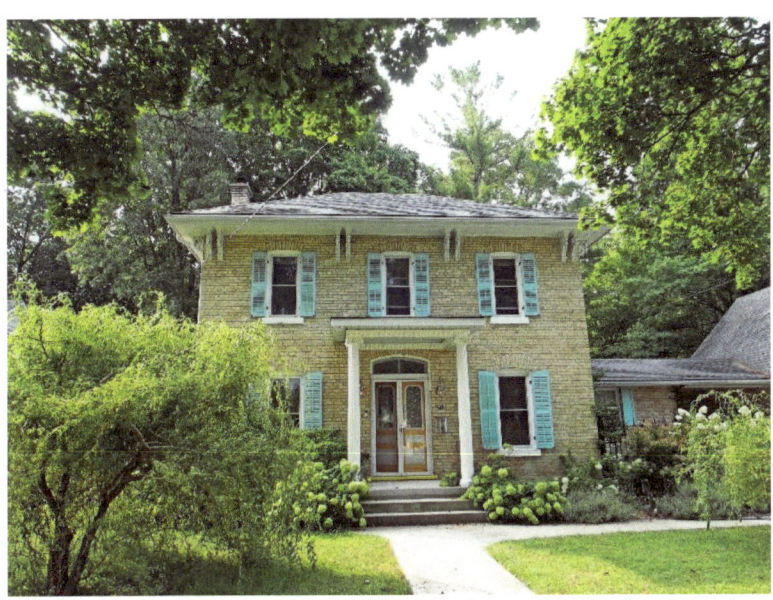

14 Kittridge Avenue West – hipped roof, cornice brackets, shutters

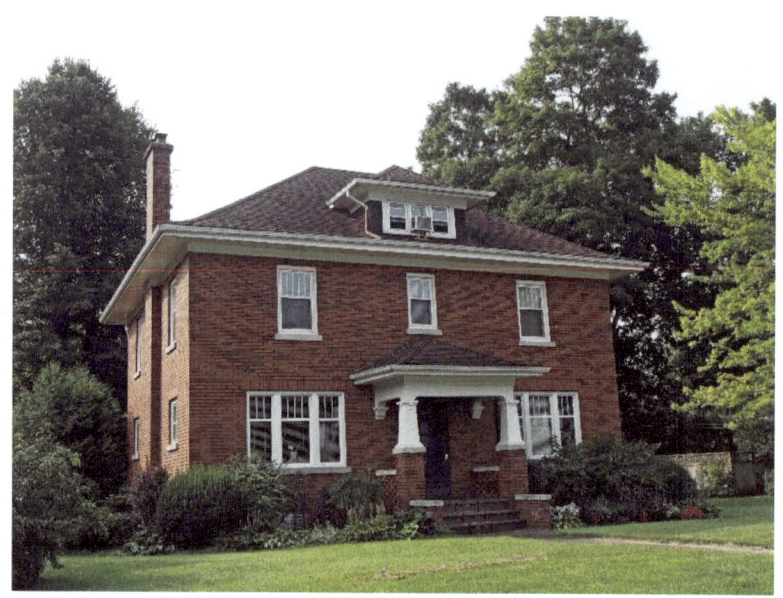

12 Kittridge Avenue West – dormer in hipped roof

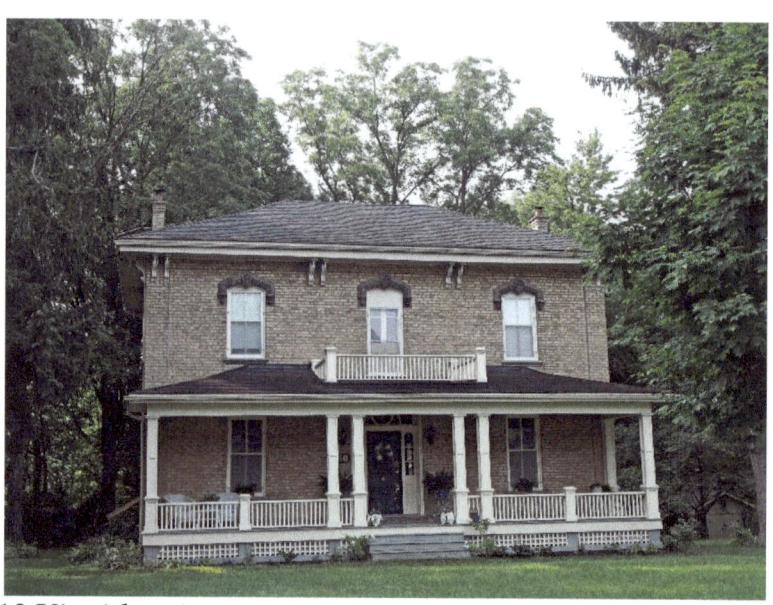

10 Kittridge Avenue West – hipped roof, paired cornice brackets, center balcony above full-width veranda

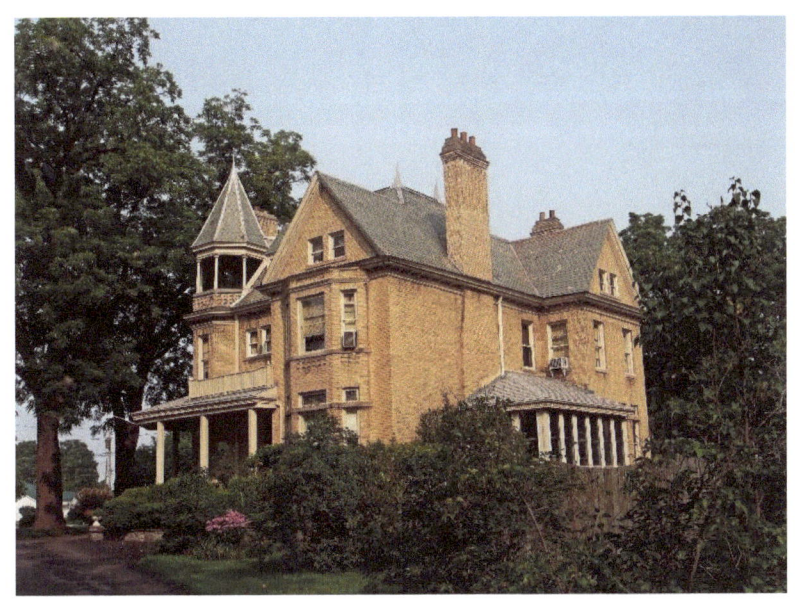

7 Kittridge Avenue West – Queen Anne - turret

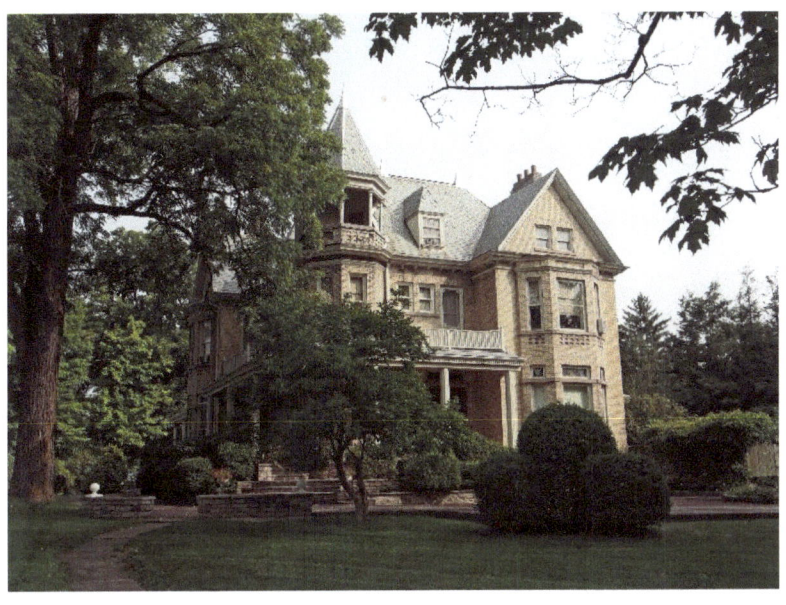

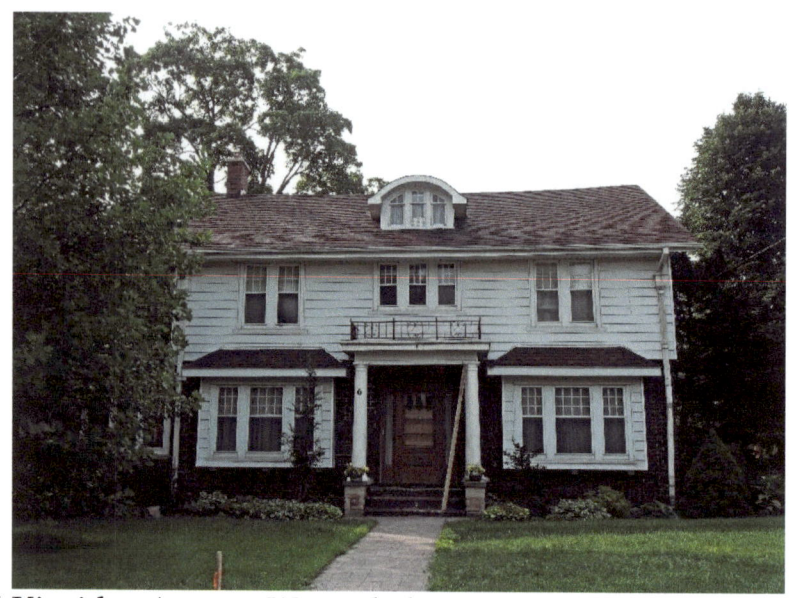

6 Kittridge Avenue West – balanced façade, bay windows

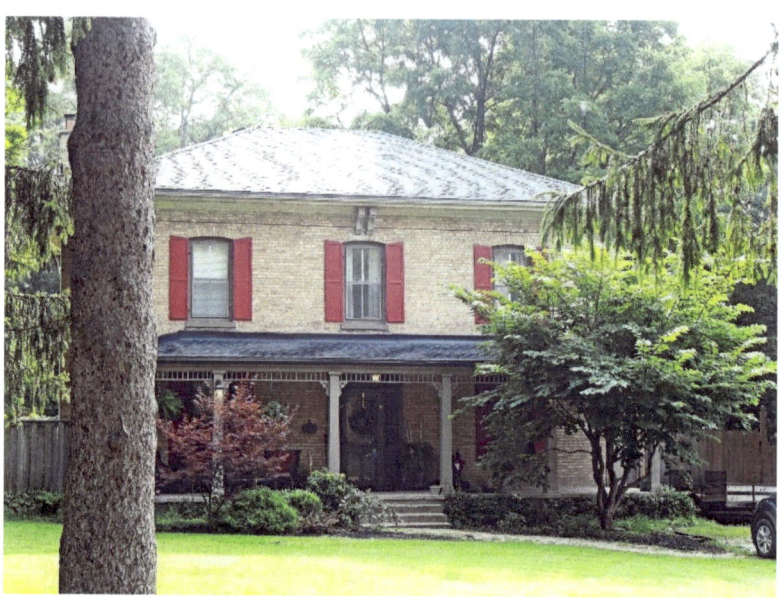

438 Victoria Street – hipped roof, cornice brackets, shutters

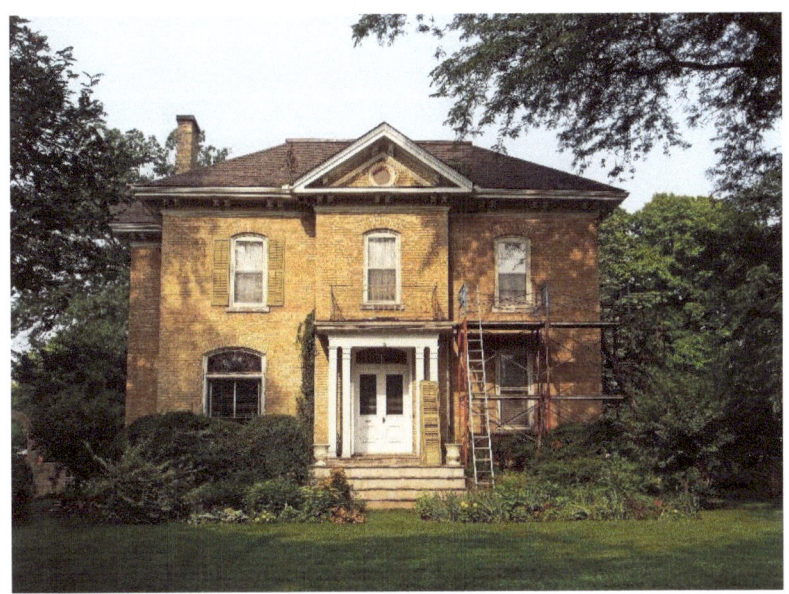

Victoria Street

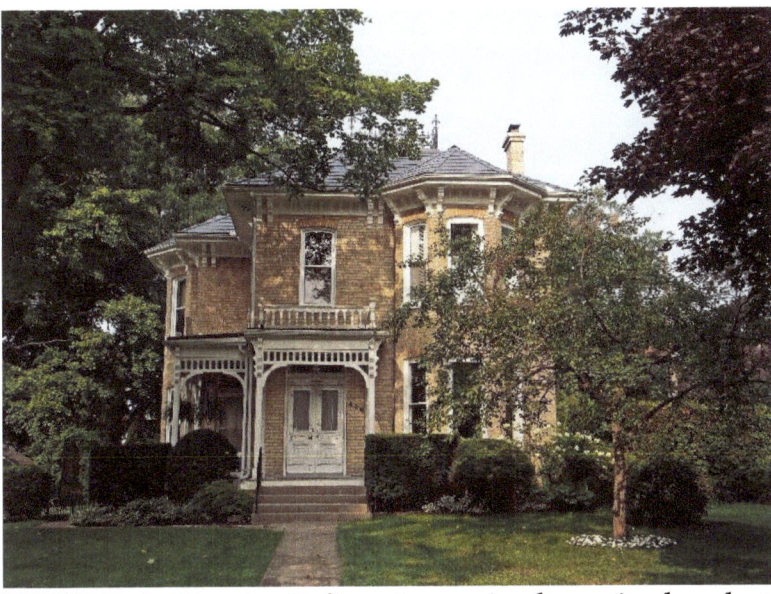

418 Victoria Street – Italianate – paired cornice brackets

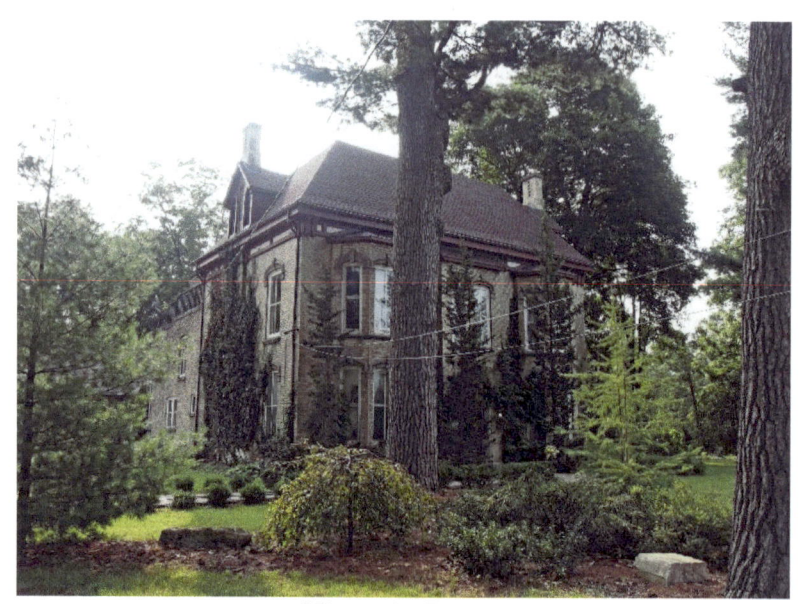

Victoria Street

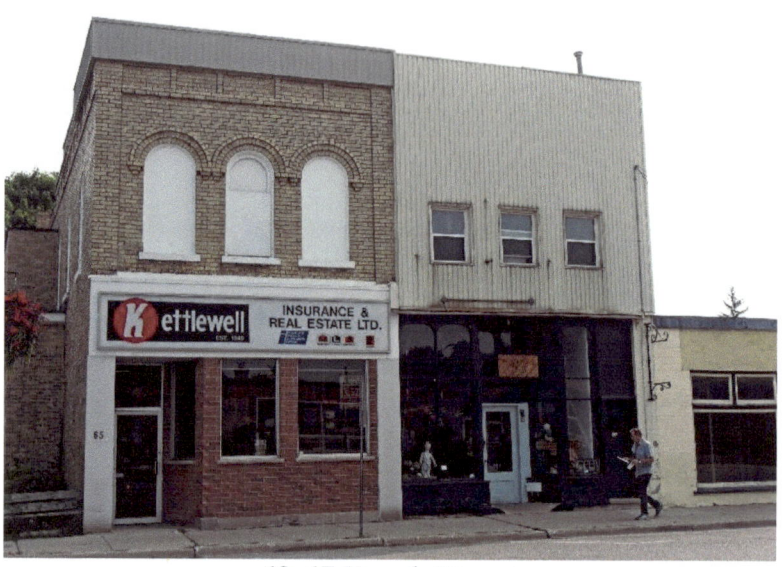

63-65 Frank Street

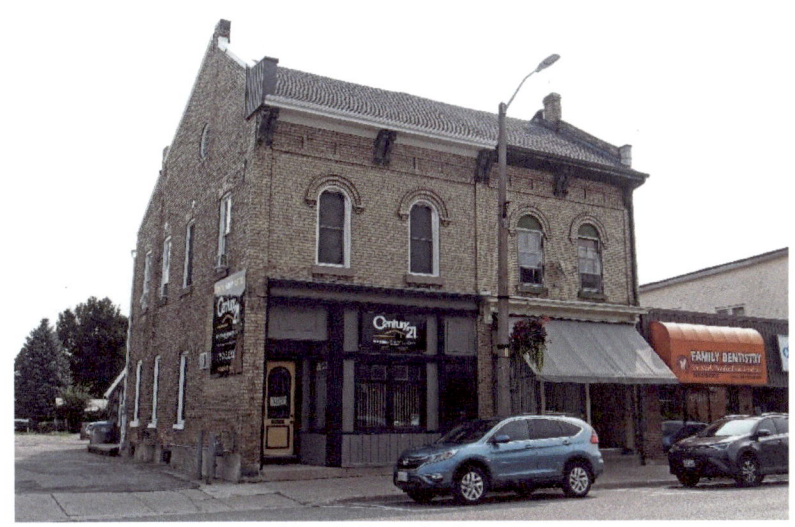

39-47 Frank Street

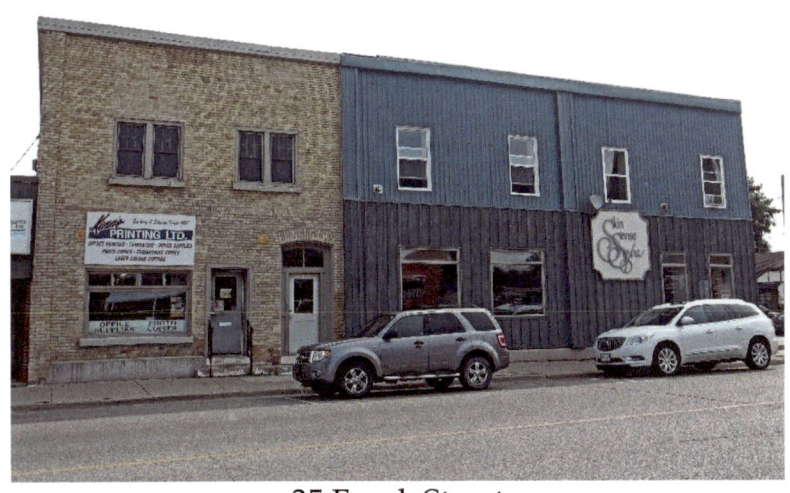

35 Frank Street

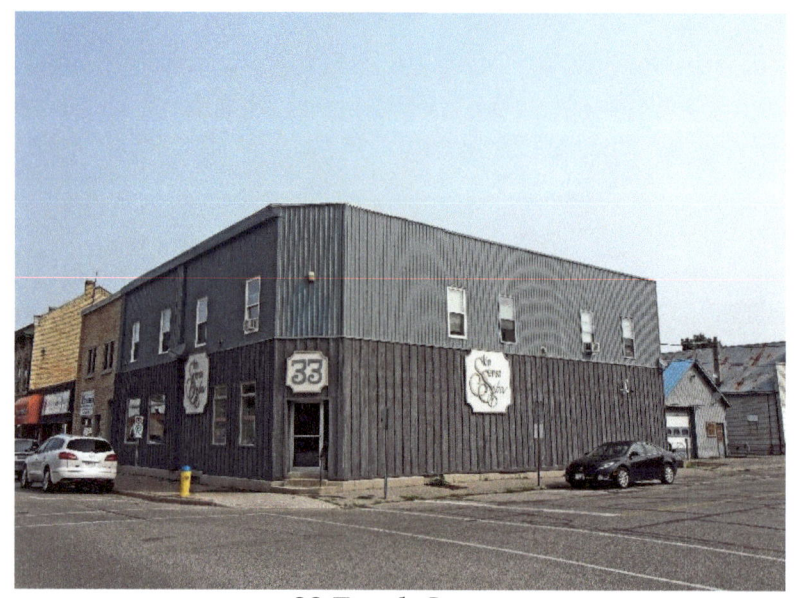

33 Frank Street

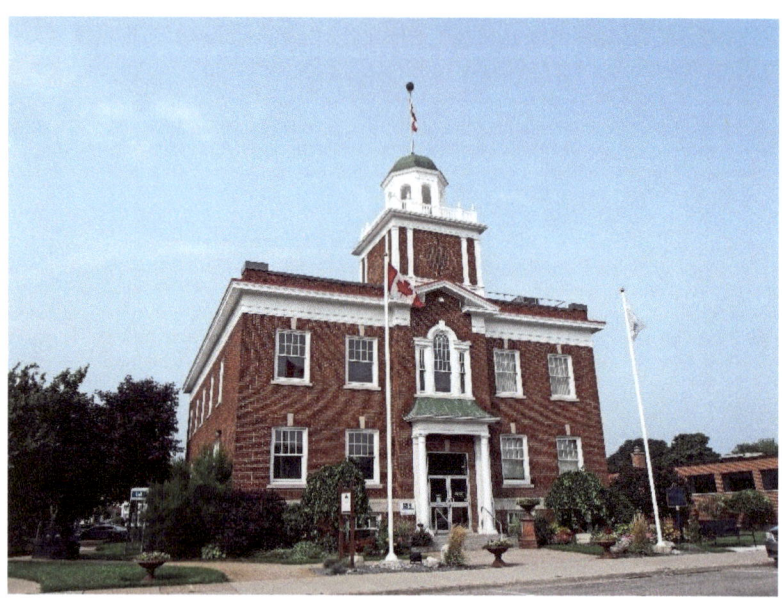

52 Frank Street - Town Hall – 1928 – reminiscent of a New England style of architecture combining beauty and utility

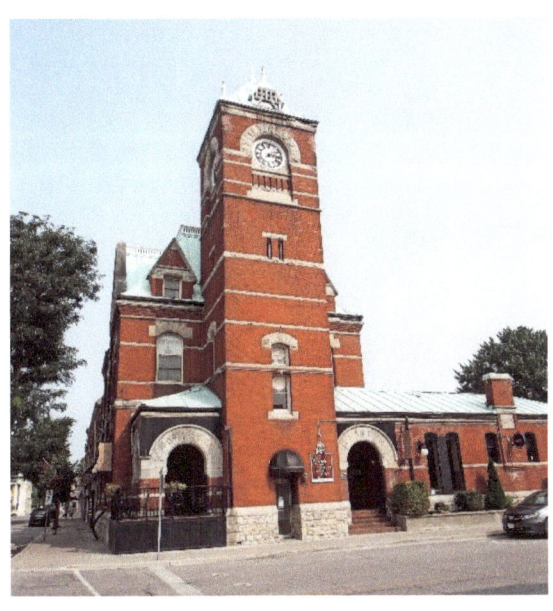

71 Frank Street – 1889 - Post Office and Customs House (until 1964), Clock Tower Inn – 1890; bell tower completed in 1901 – designed in the "Dominion" architectural style

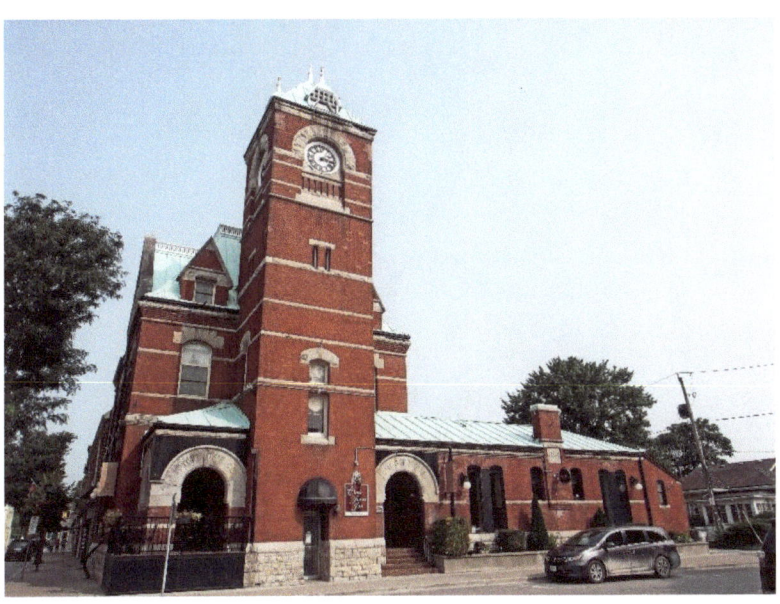

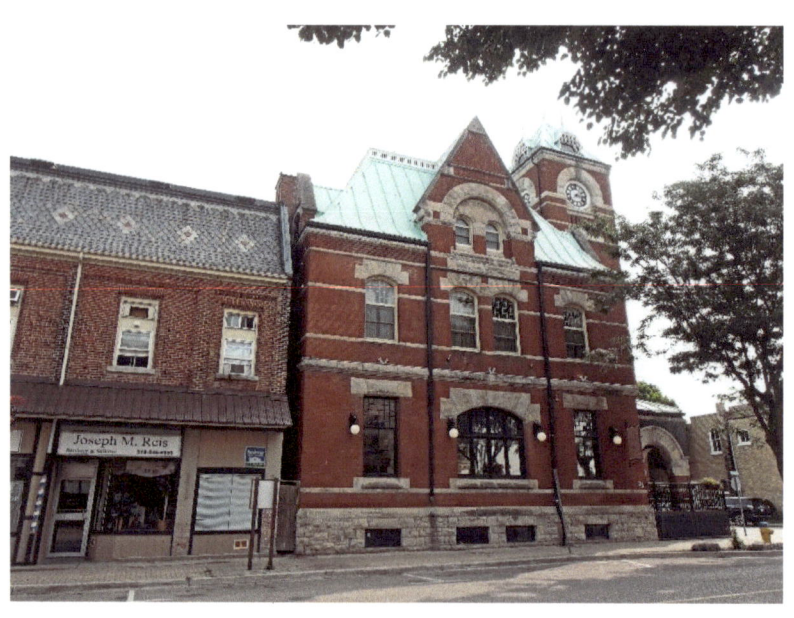

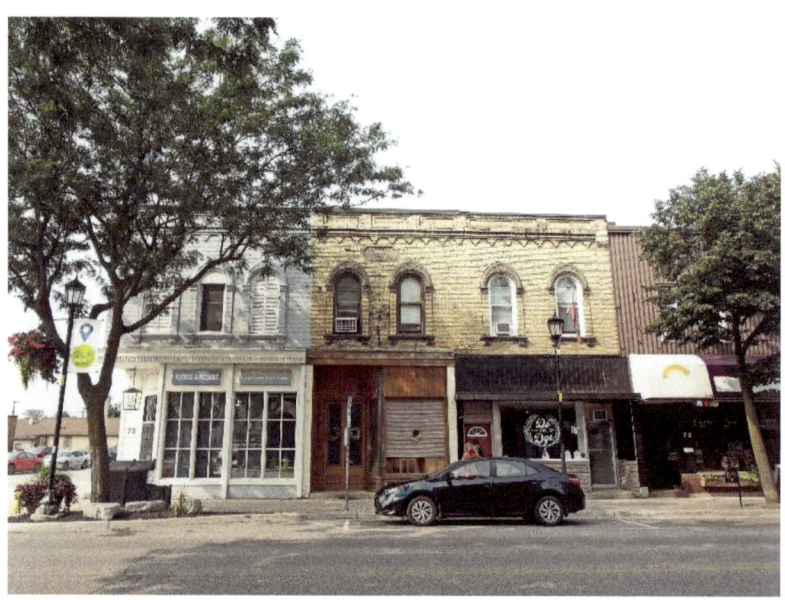

72-78 Frank Street

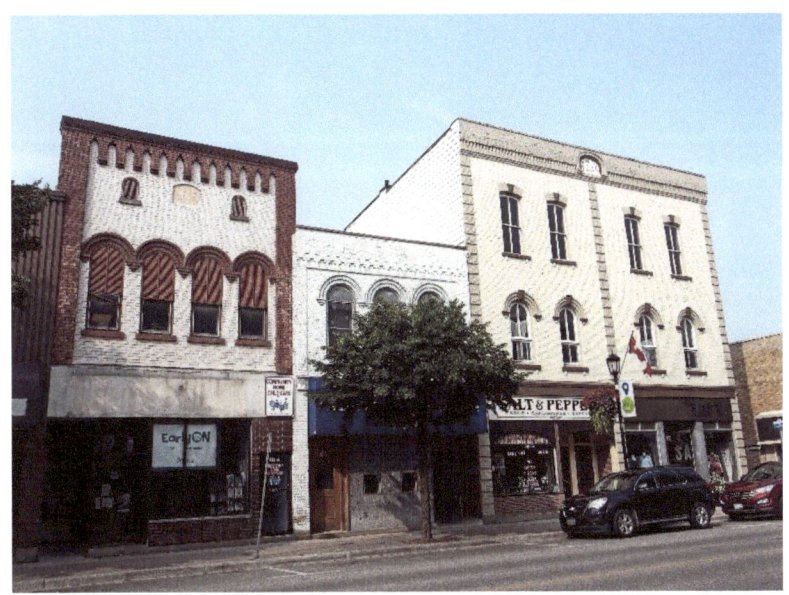

80 Frank Street – Robert McLarty Building – 1876 – decorative cornice; 84-86 Frank Street – Lochfine Block – A.D. 1872 – keystones, drip molds, quoins

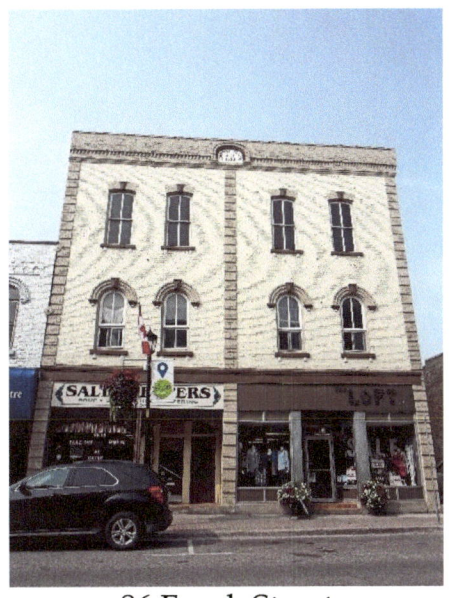

86 Frank Street

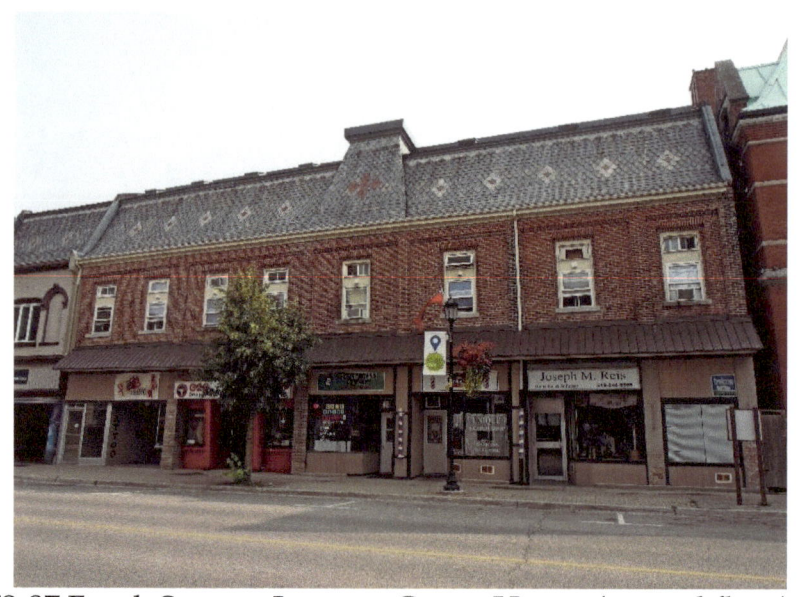

79-87 Frank Street – Lyceum Opera House (second floor) – opened in 1891 - seating capacity of 600

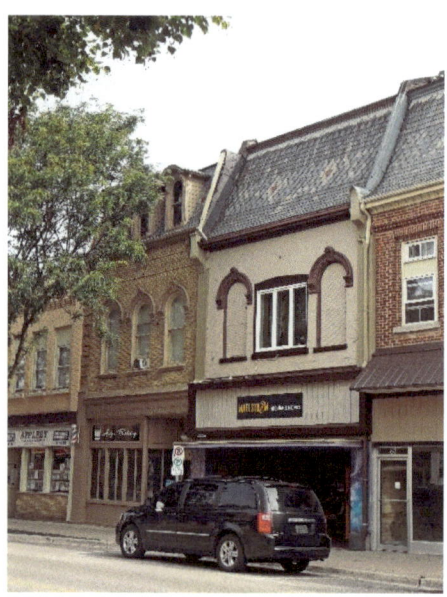

89 Frank Street

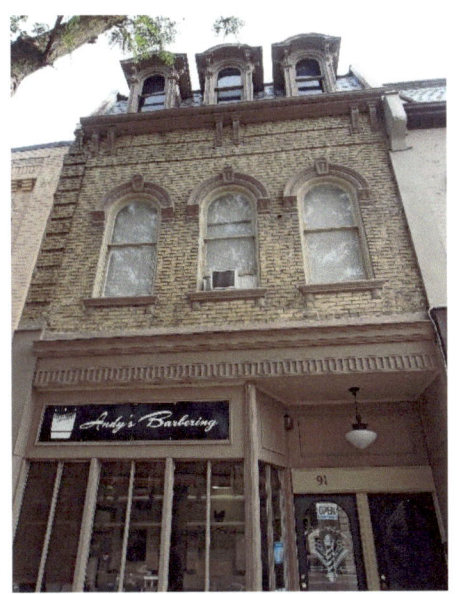

91 Frank Street

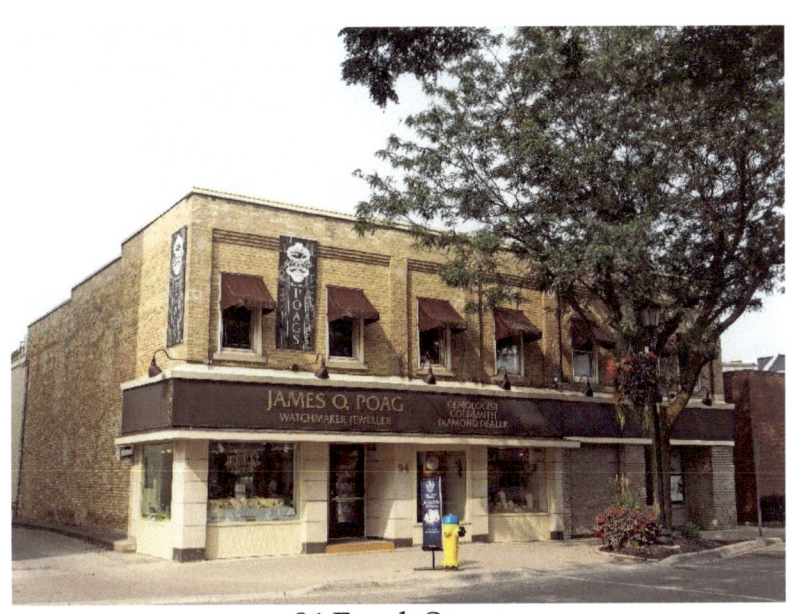

94 Frank Street

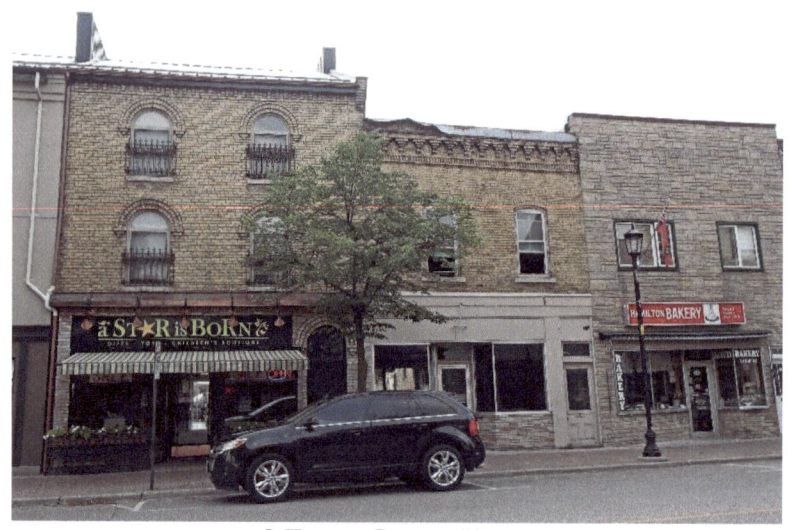

8 Front Street West

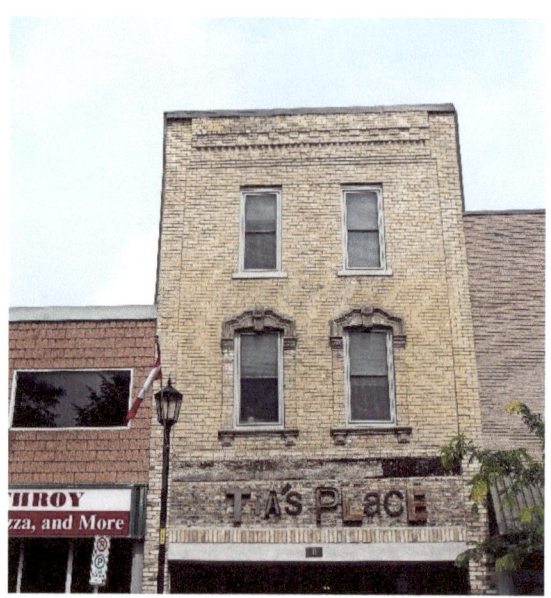

11 Front Street West – decorative cornice

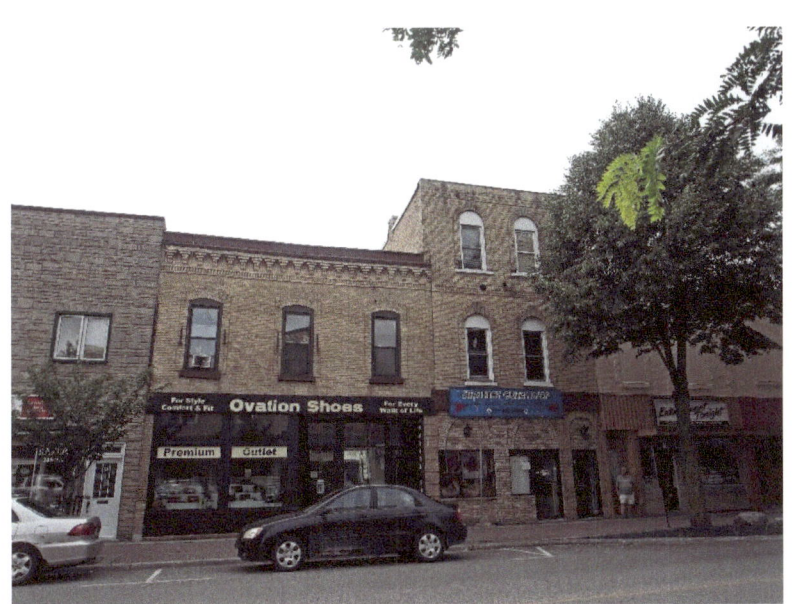

14 Front Street West

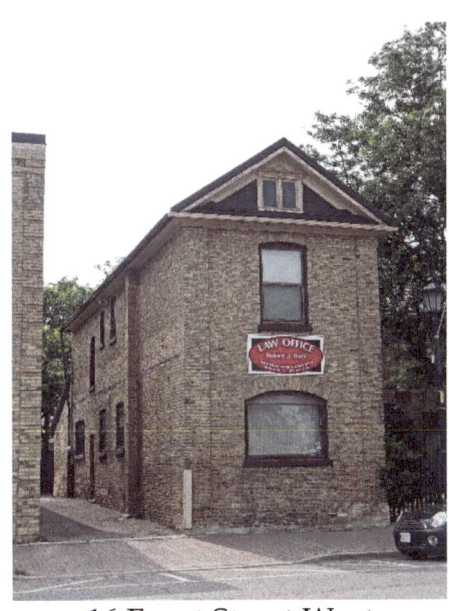

16 Front Street West

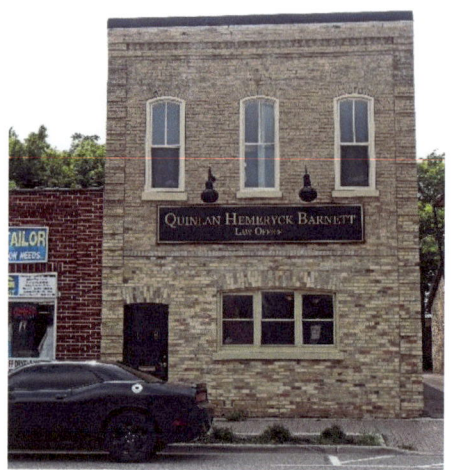

18 Front Street West

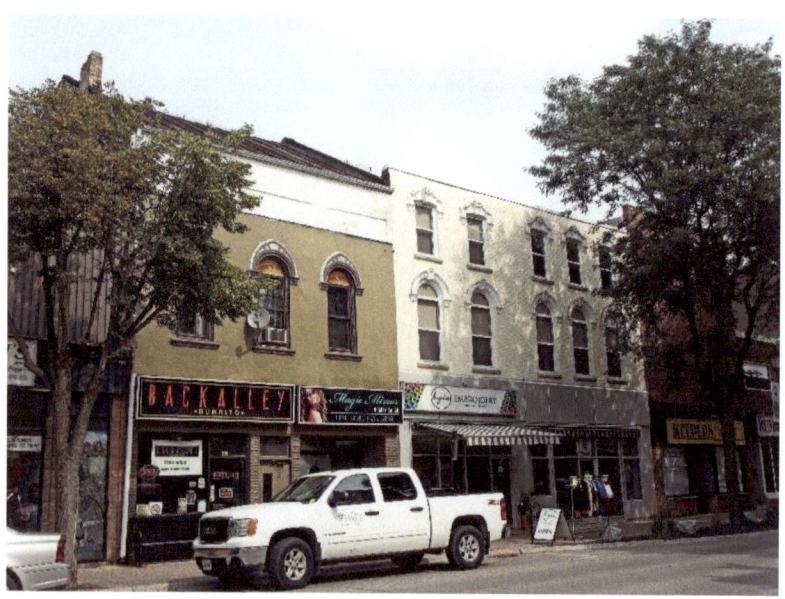

19-23 Front Street West

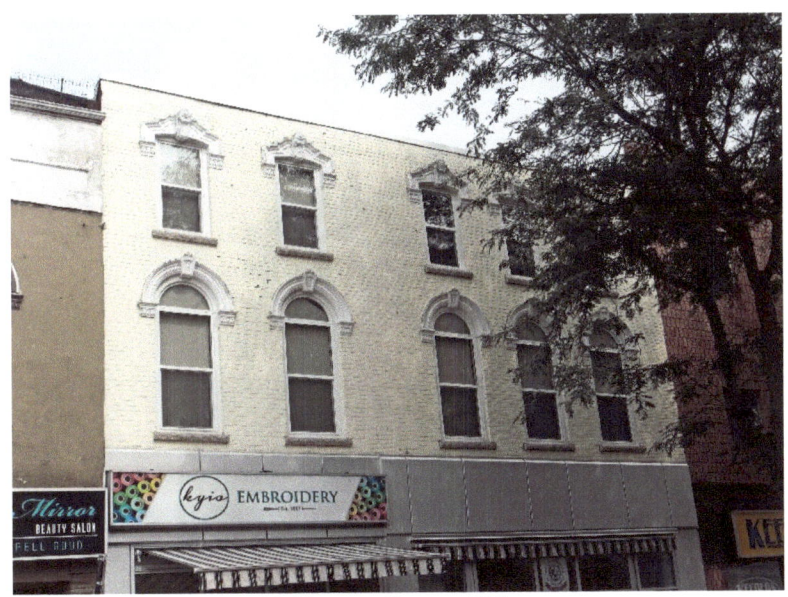

19 Front Street West

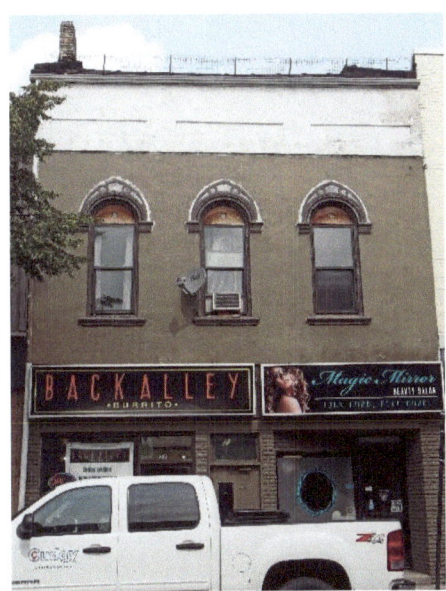

23 Front Street West

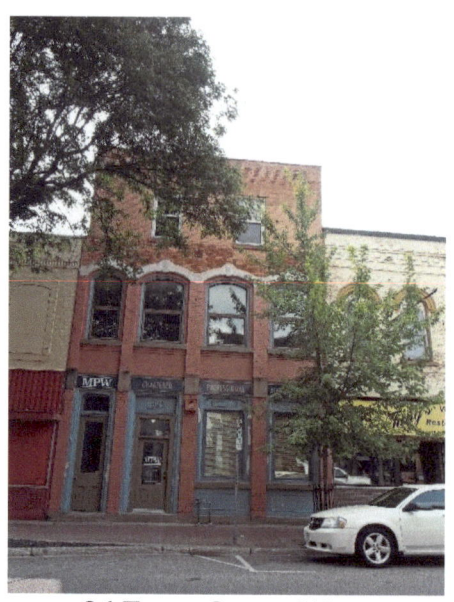
26 Front Street West

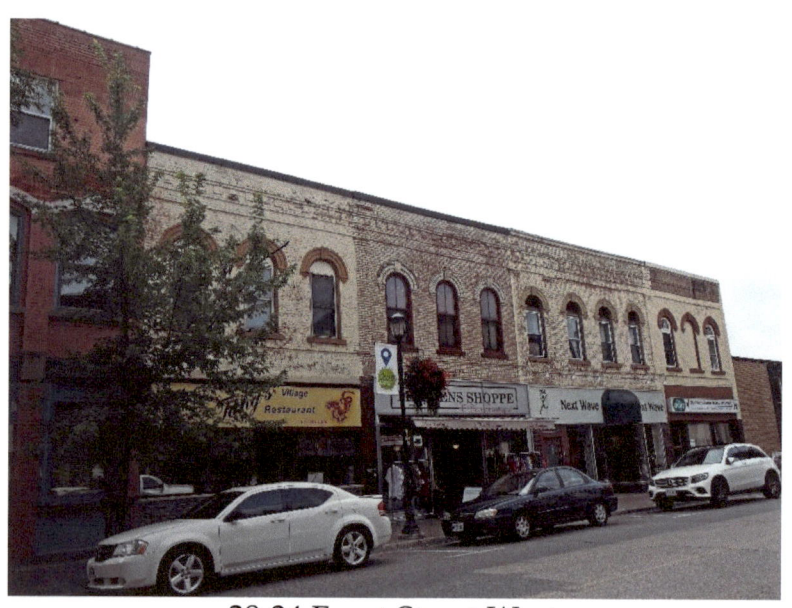
28-34 Front Street West

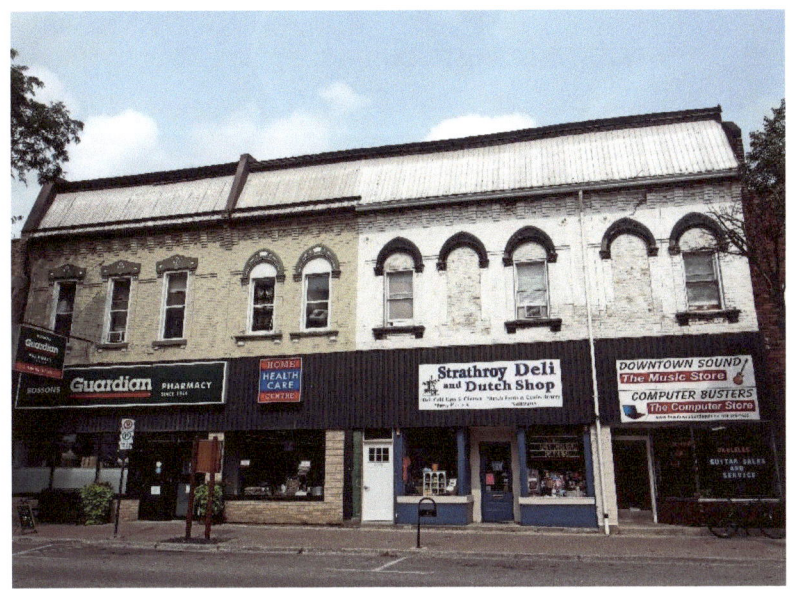

31-35 Front Street West
35 Front Street West has been a drug store since the 1880s.

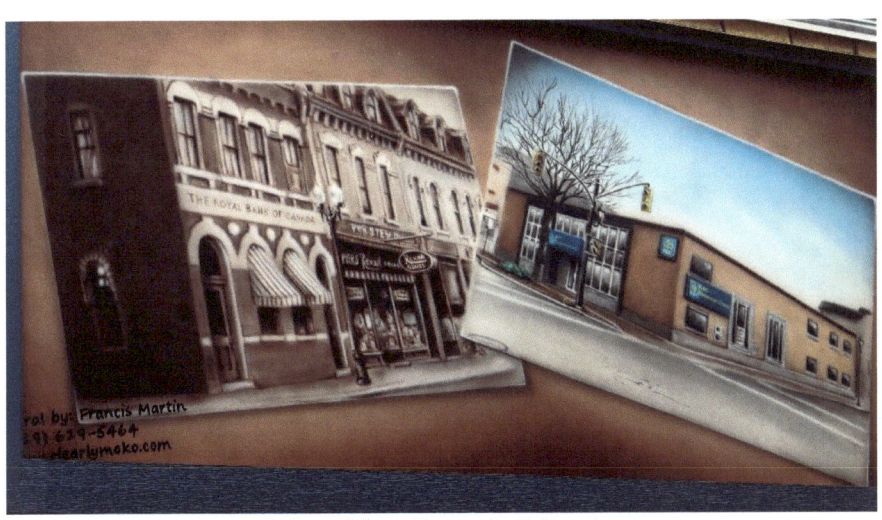

Mural by Francis Martin

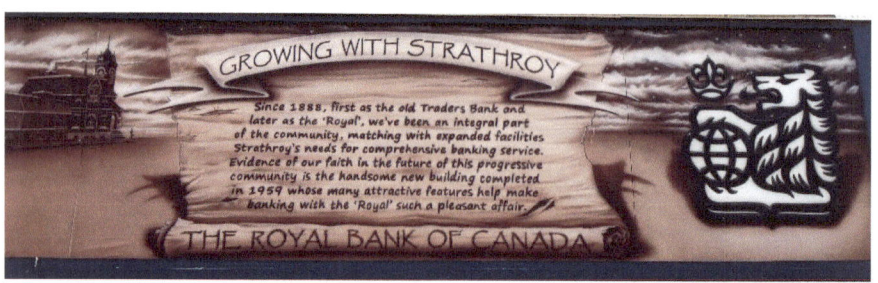

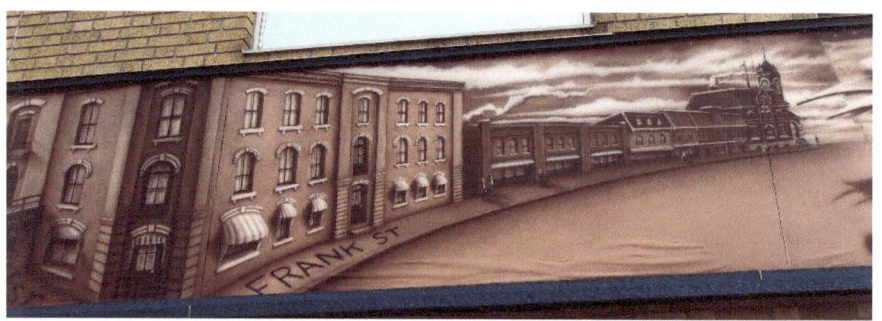

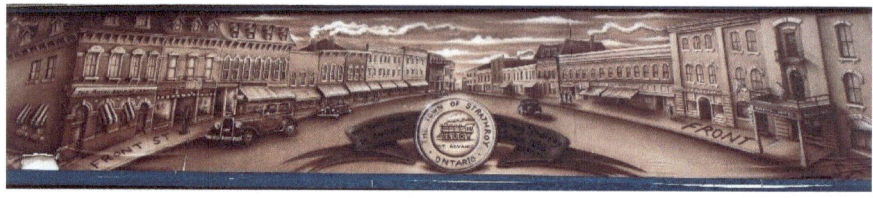

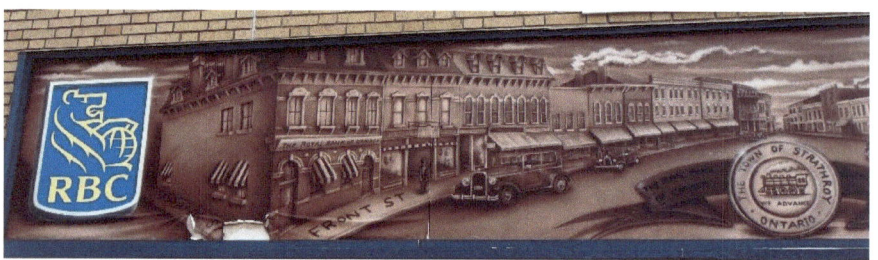

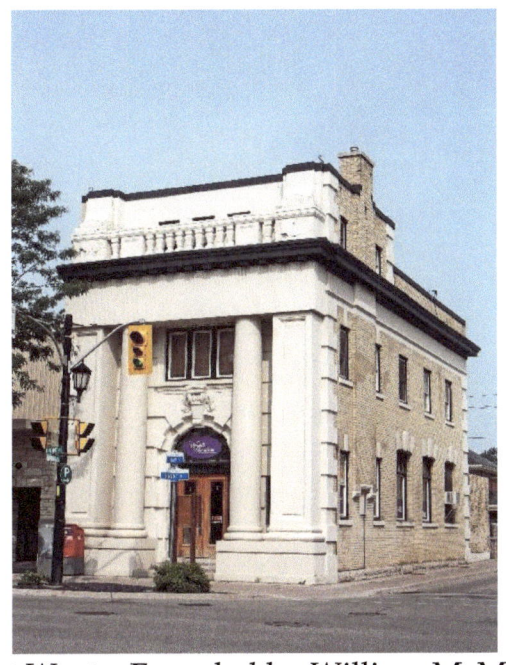

51 Front Street West – Founded by William McMaster just before the Confederation of Canada in 1867, the Canadian Bank of Commerce quickly became the dominant financial institution in the country. In 1883, this building on the corner of Frank and Front Streets, was constructed. It features a Doric inspired front with vertical pillars in the Classical Greek style.

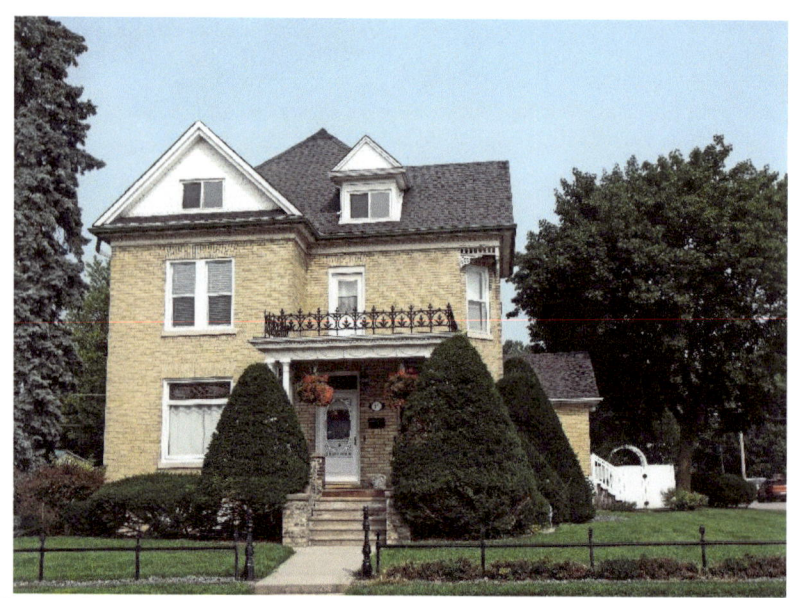
93 Front Street – dormer, iron cresting on second-floor balcony

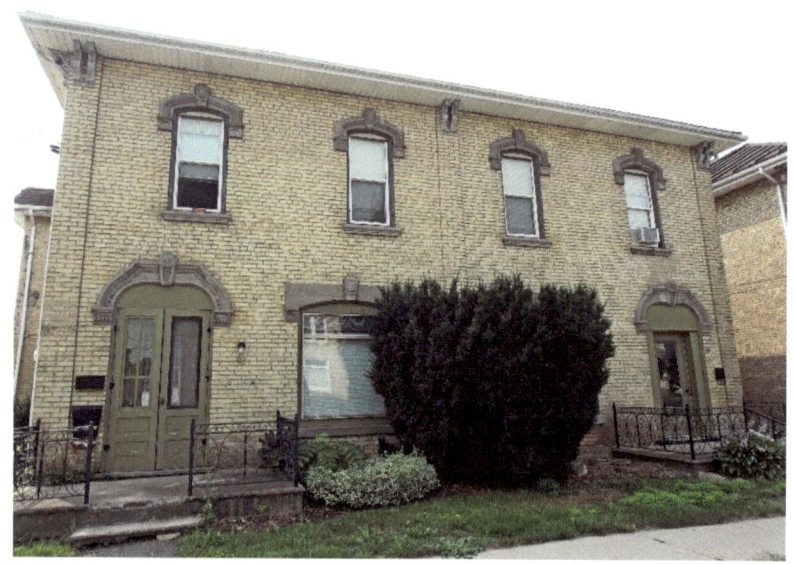
92-94 Front Street – keystones, drip molds, paired cornice brackets

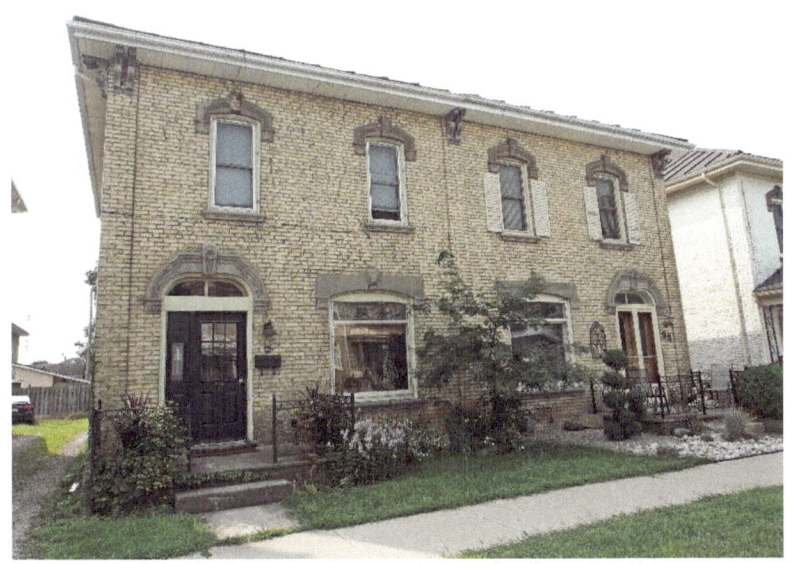

96-98 Front Street – identical to 92-94

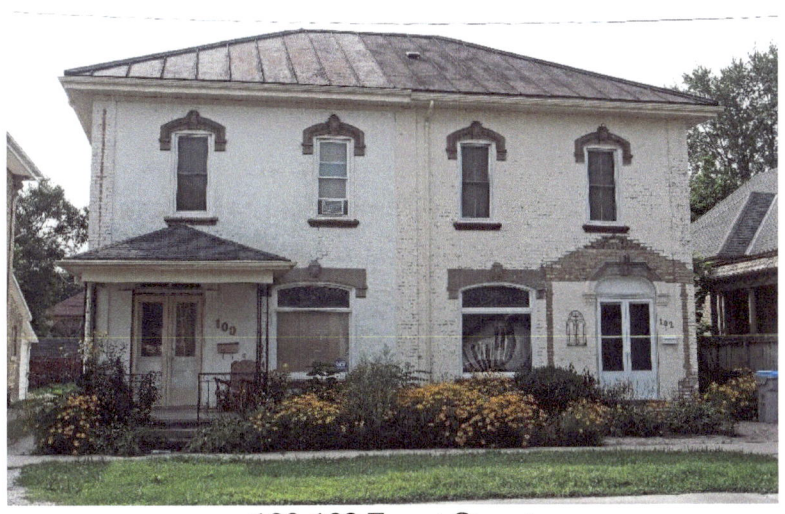

100-102 Front Street

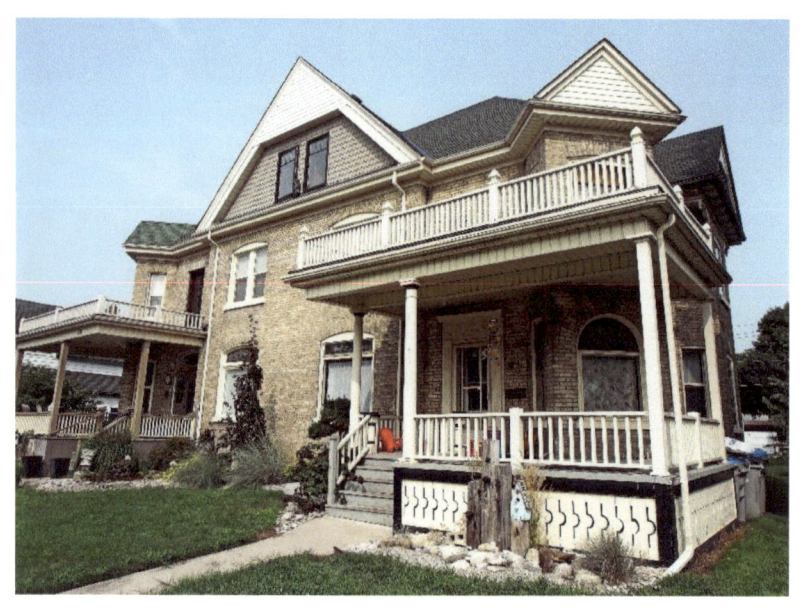

97-99 Front Street

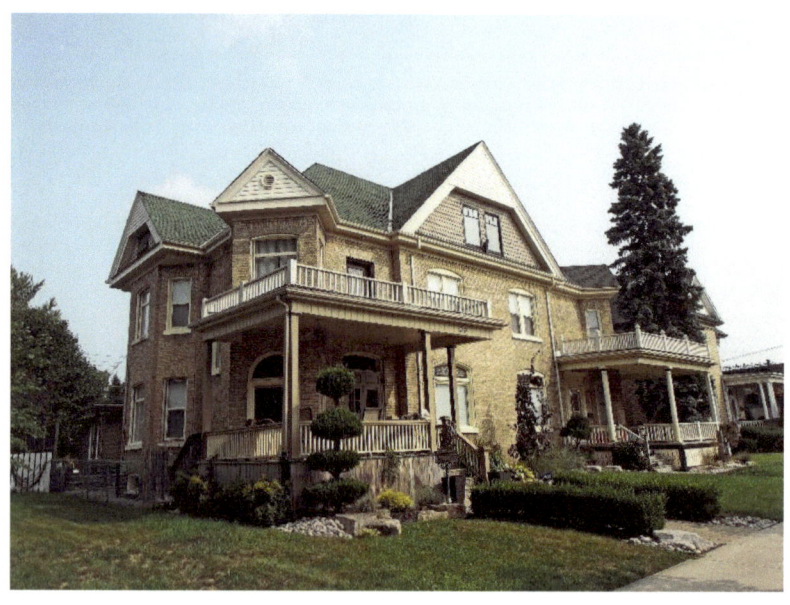

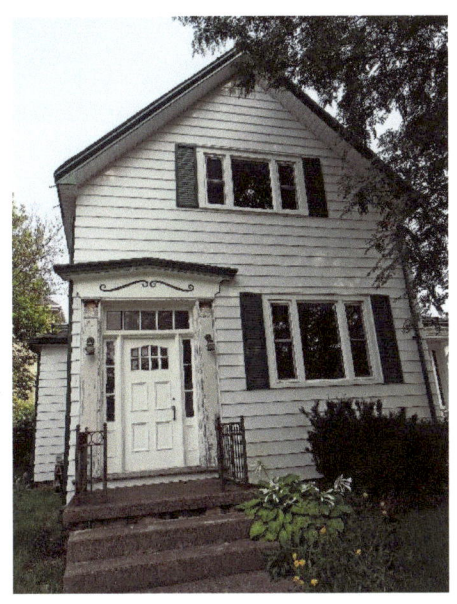

105 Front Street

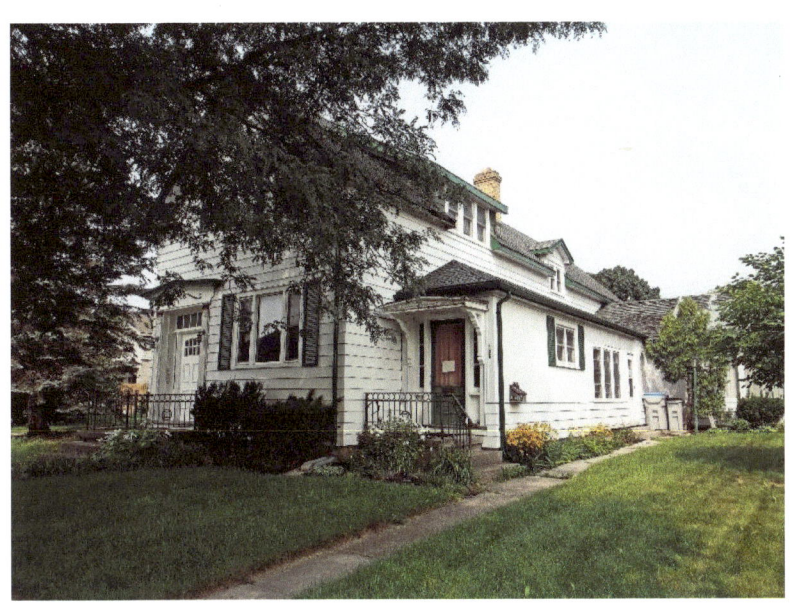

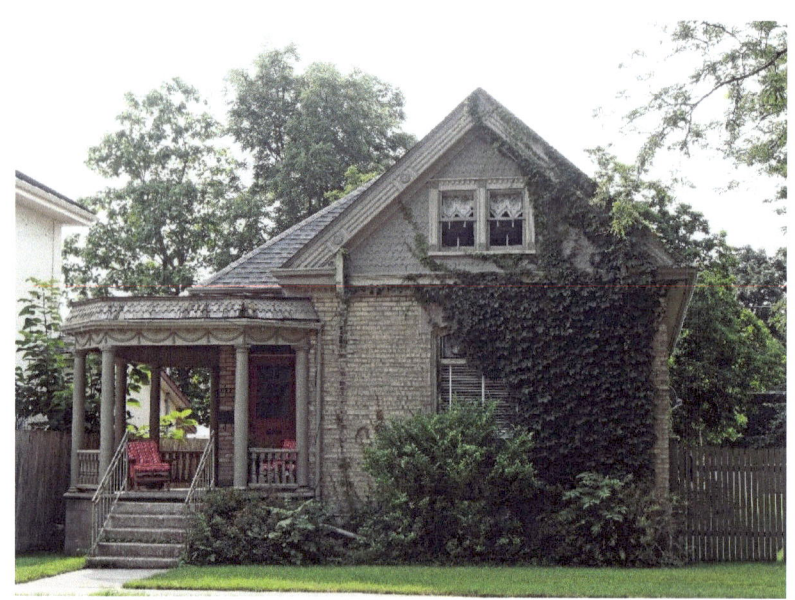
106 Front Street – wraparound veranda

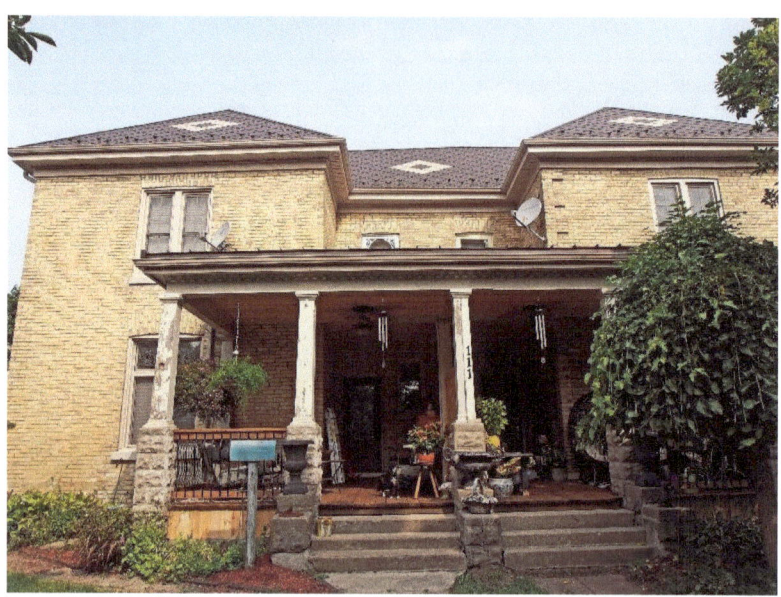
109-111 Front Street

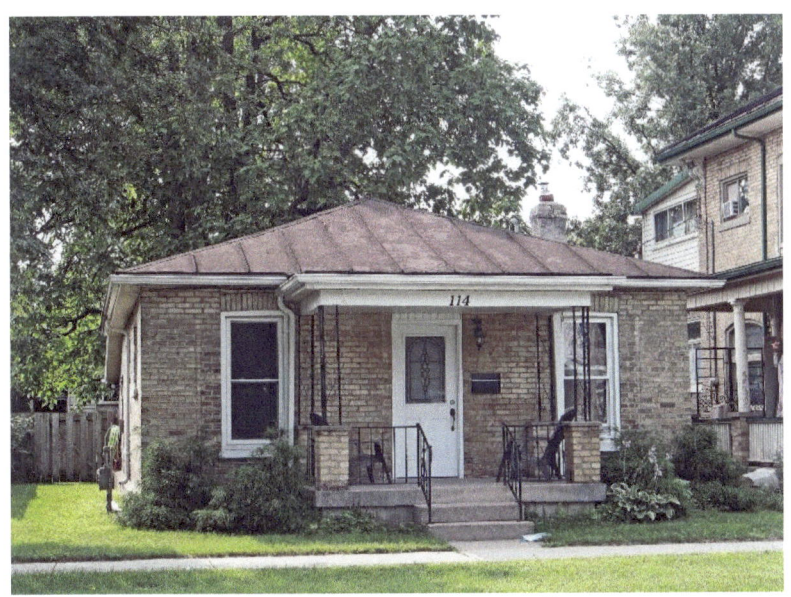

114 Front Street – Regency Cottage

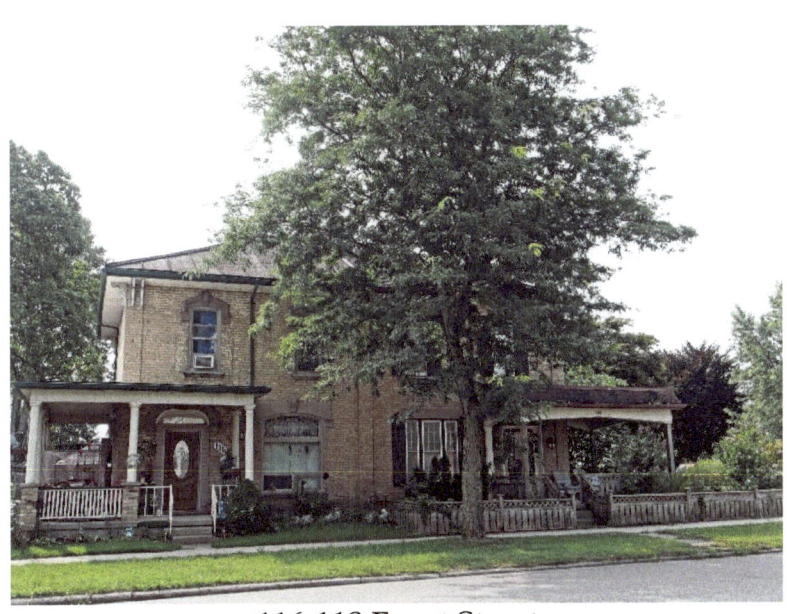

116-118 Front Street

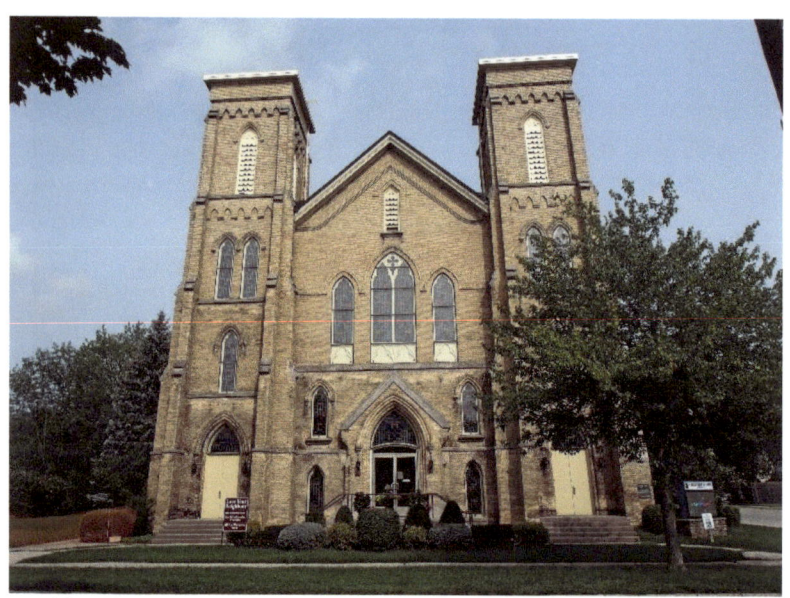

131 Front Street West – Strathroy United Church - From 1834 to 1840 pioneers worshipped outside or in the largest log building available in Adelaide Township, mostly in James Cooper's cabin. In 1840, a log church was erected on the 4th line South in Adelaide Township and named the Wesleyan Methodist Church. In 1851 a white frame church was built in the center of Strathroy on Front Street. In 1861, a larger frame church was built on the corner of North and Maria Streets. Originally there were five denominations of Methodists in Ontario: Wesleyan, New Connexion, Methodist Episcopal, Primitive and Bible Christian. In 1874, a Union of the Wesleyan and New Connexion Methodists took place, and the united body was called the Methodist Church of Canada. In 1879 the brick church on the corner of Front and Maria Streets was built. In 1884, all strains of Methodism united and were named the Methodist Church. The union of the Congregationalists, and part of the Presbyterians and Methodists joined together in 1925 and became the United Church of Canada. This church was renamed Strathroy United Church.

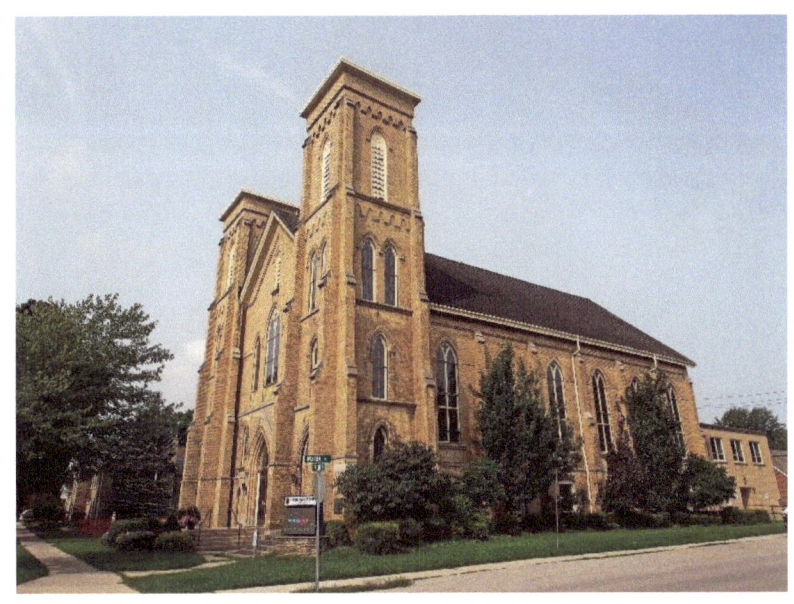

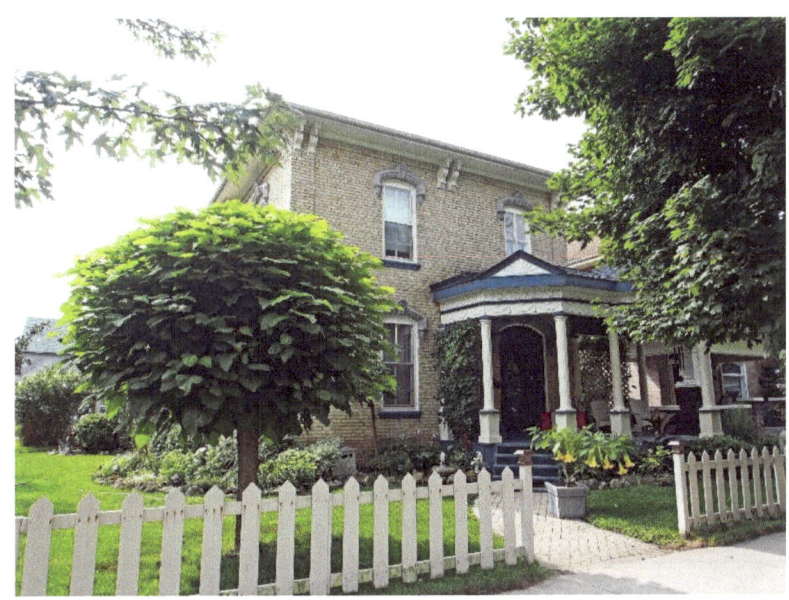

132 Front Street

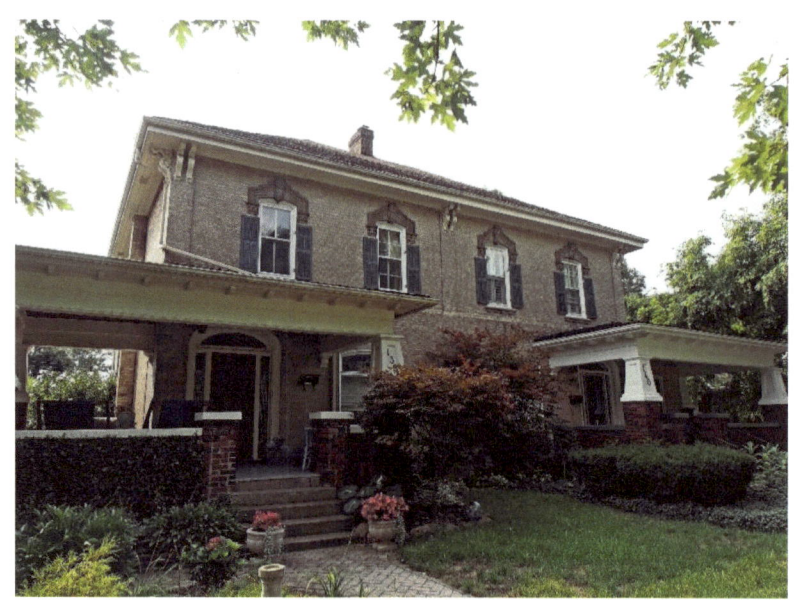

138-140 Front Street

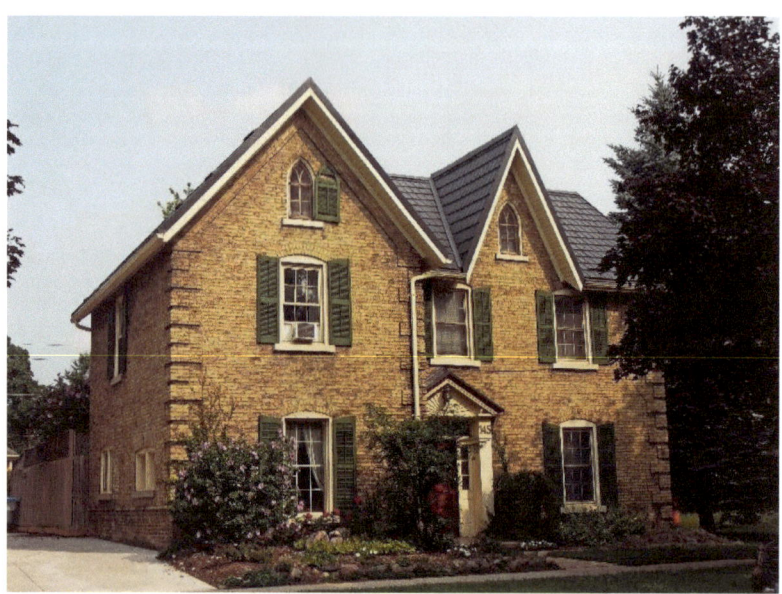

145 Front Street – Gothic – corner quoins, shutters

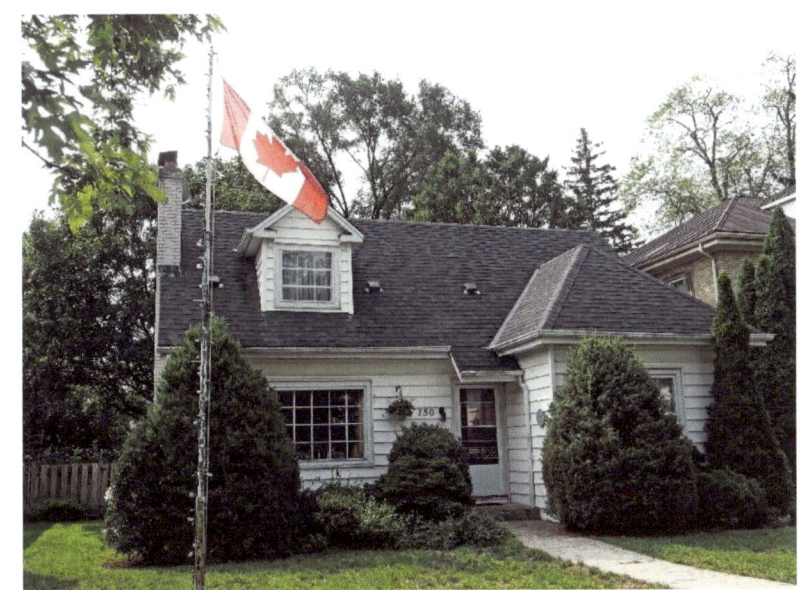

150 Front Street

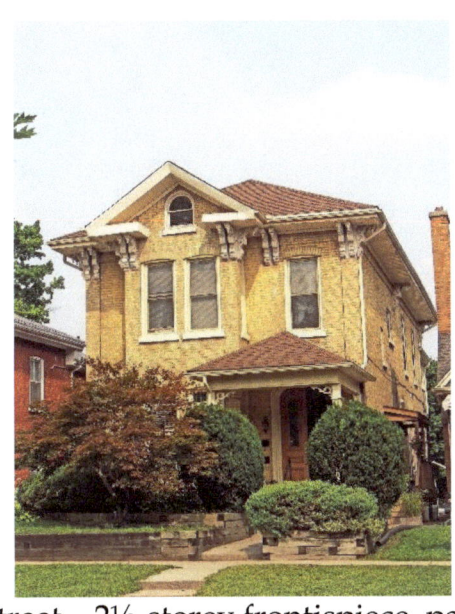

153 Front Street – 2½-storey frontispiece, paired cornice brackets

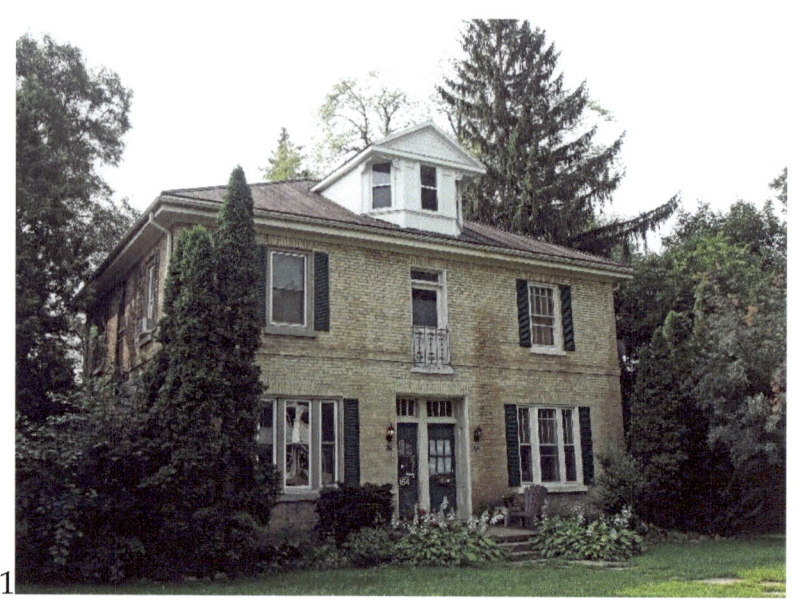

154-156 Front Street - dormer

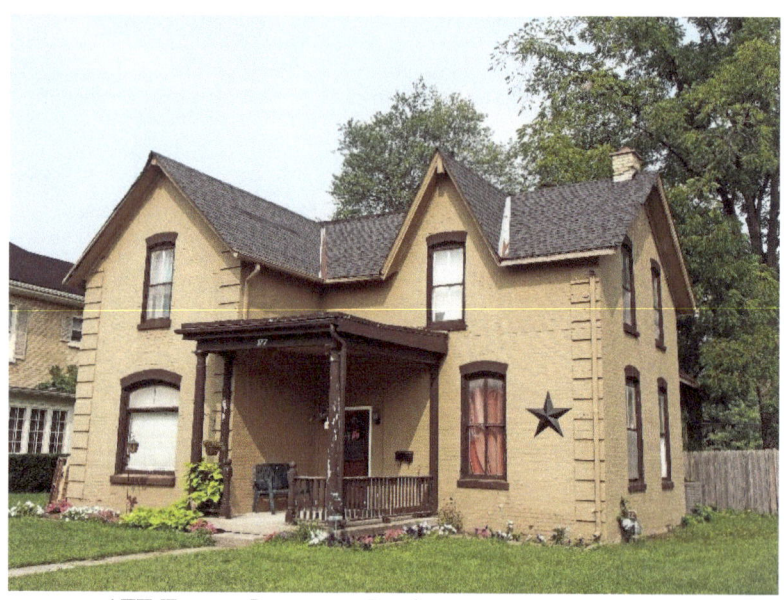

177 Front Street – Gothic – corner quoins

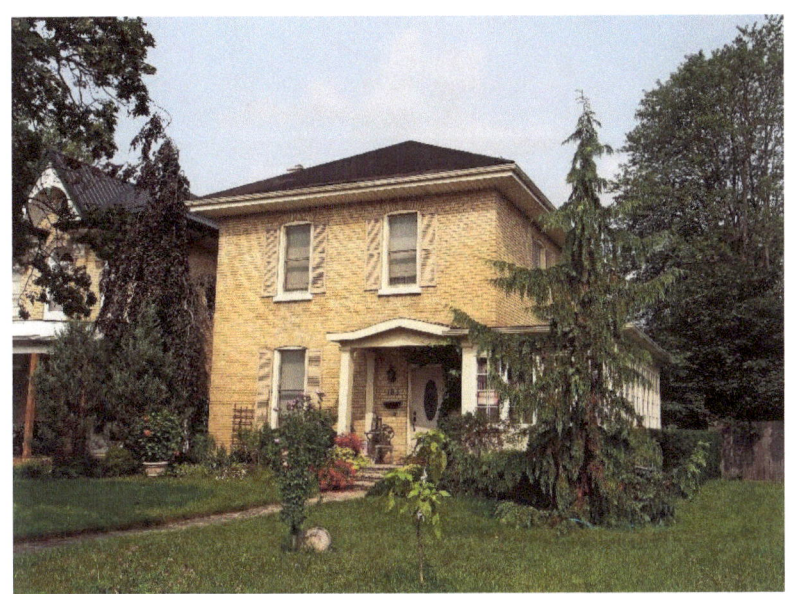

183 Front Street – hipped roof

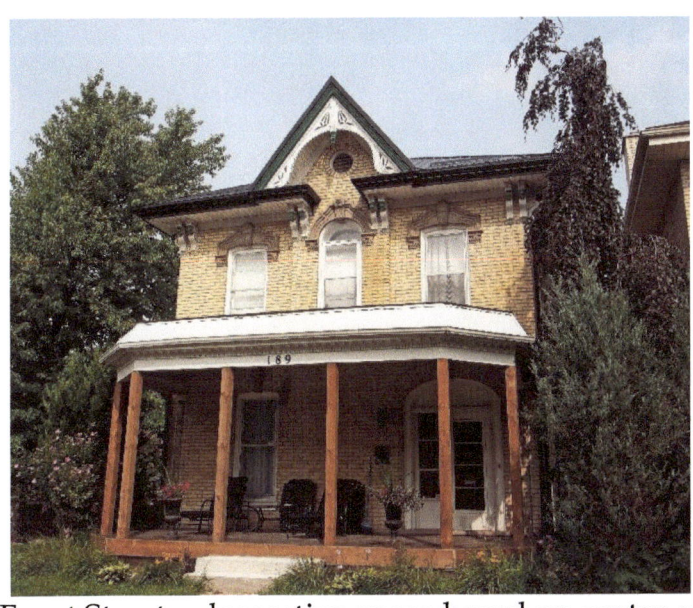

189 Front Street – decorative verge board on center gable, paired cornice brackets

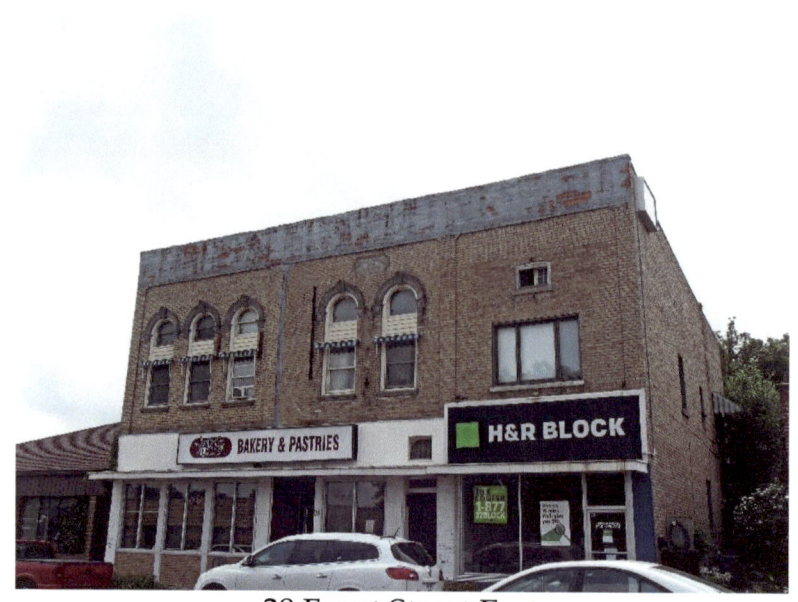

28 Front Street East

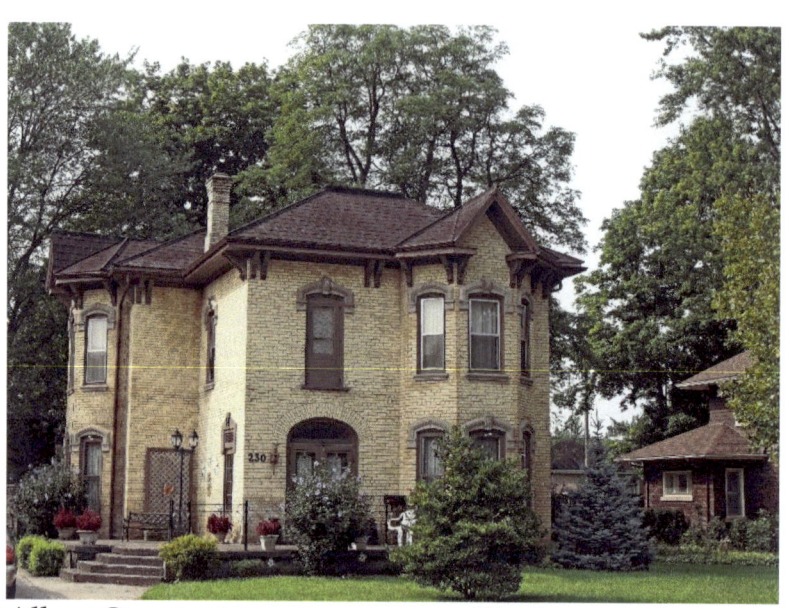

230 Albert Street – two-storey tower-like bay windows, paired cornice brackets

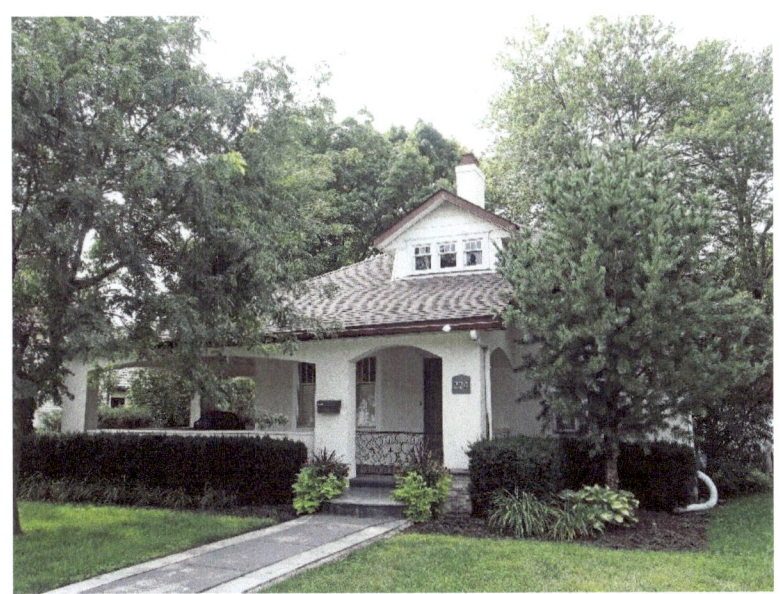

224 Albert Street

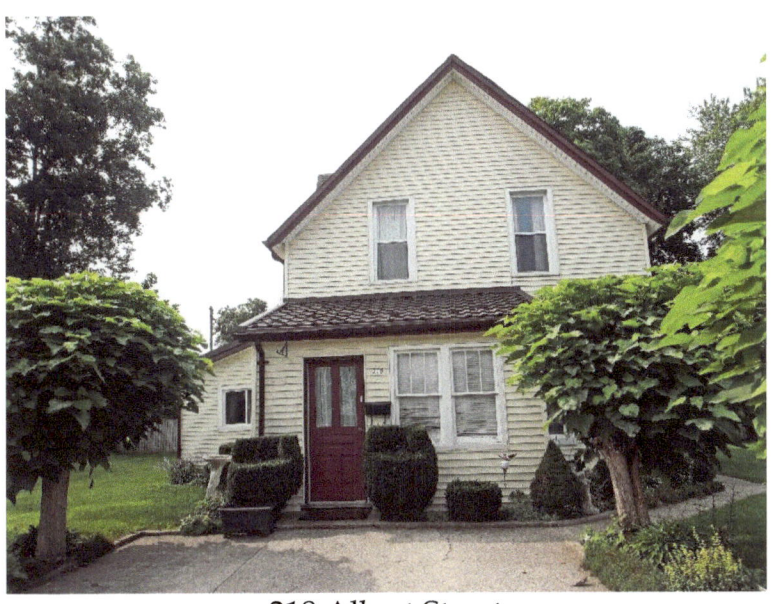

218 Albert Street

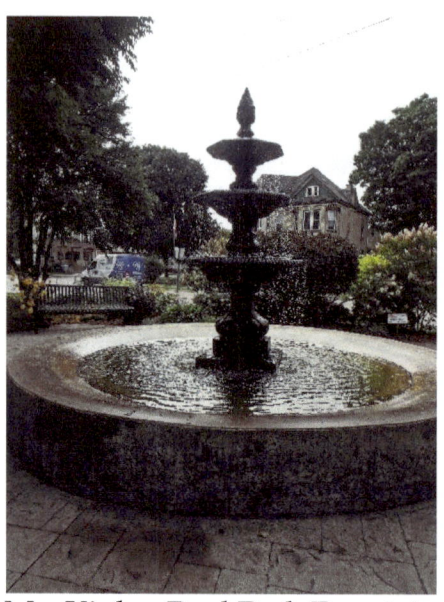

MacKinlay Paul Park Fountain

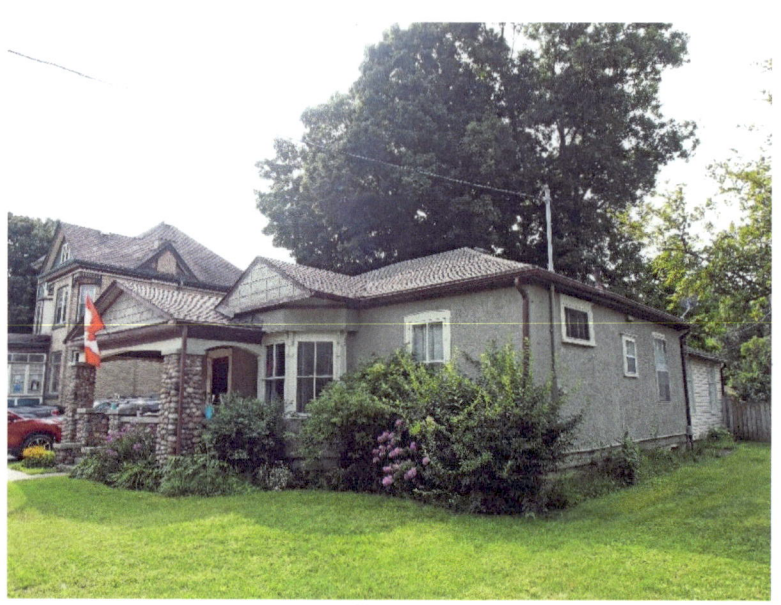

210 Albert Street

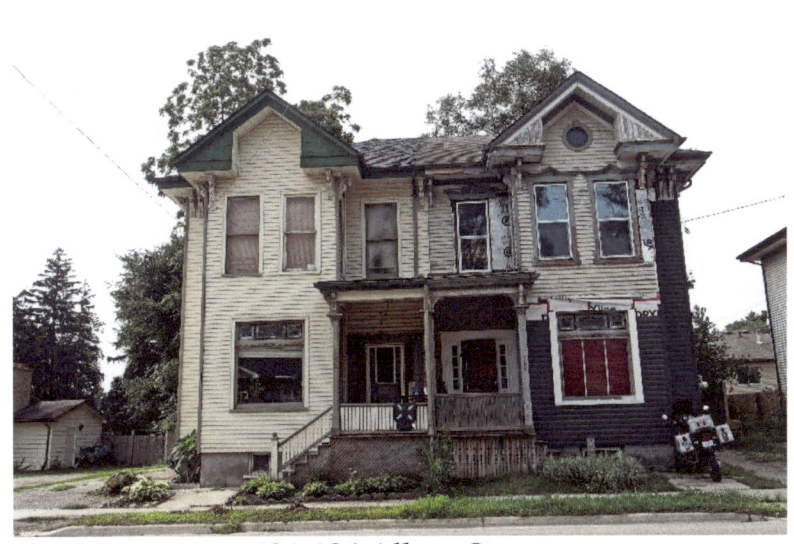
184-186 Albert Street

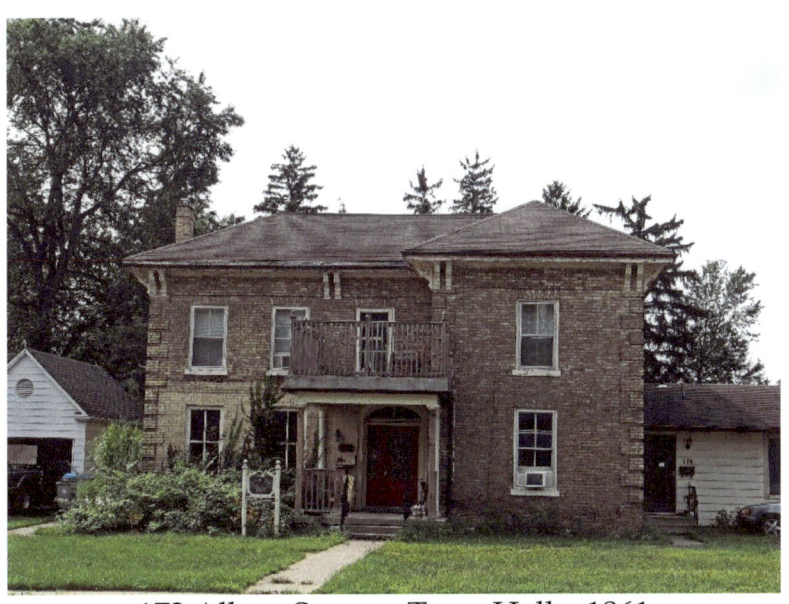
172 Albert Street – Terra Hall – 1861

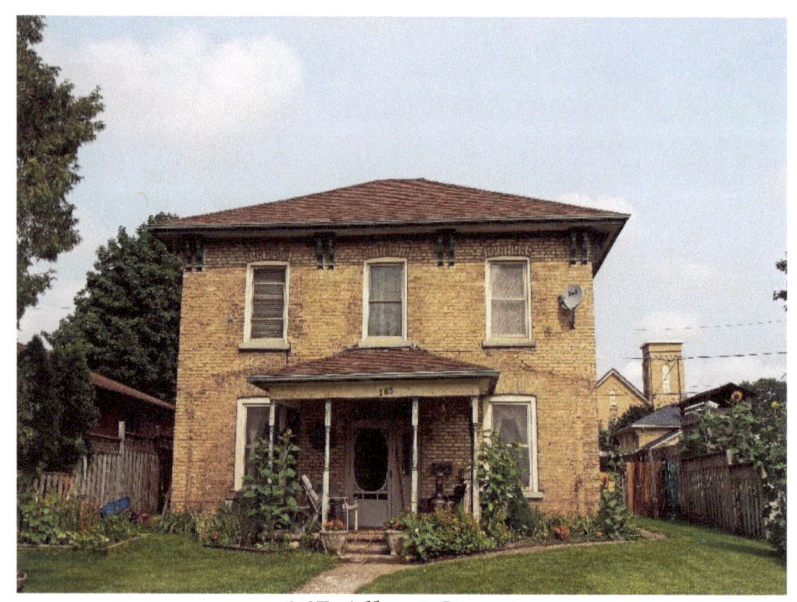

165 Albert Street

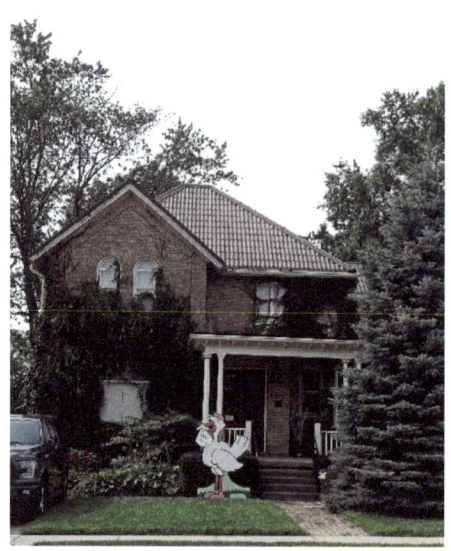

162 Albert Street

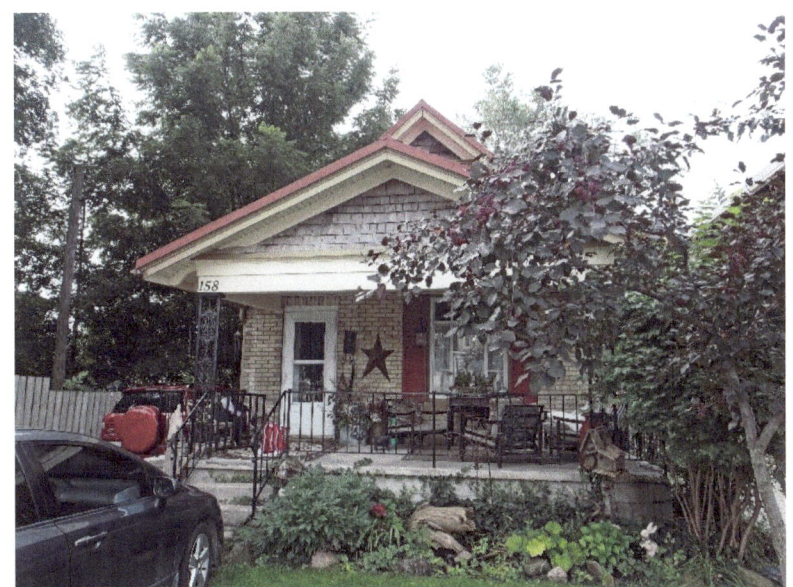

158 Albert Street

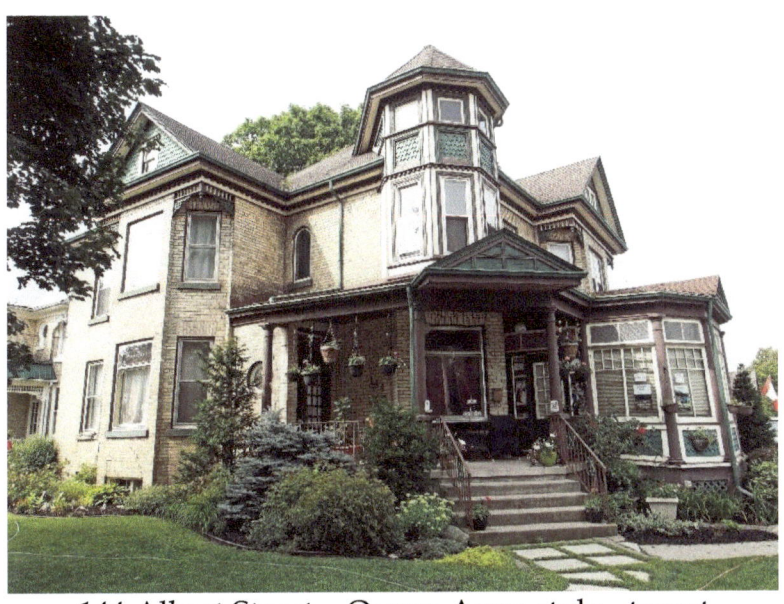

144 Albert Street – Queen Anne style - turret

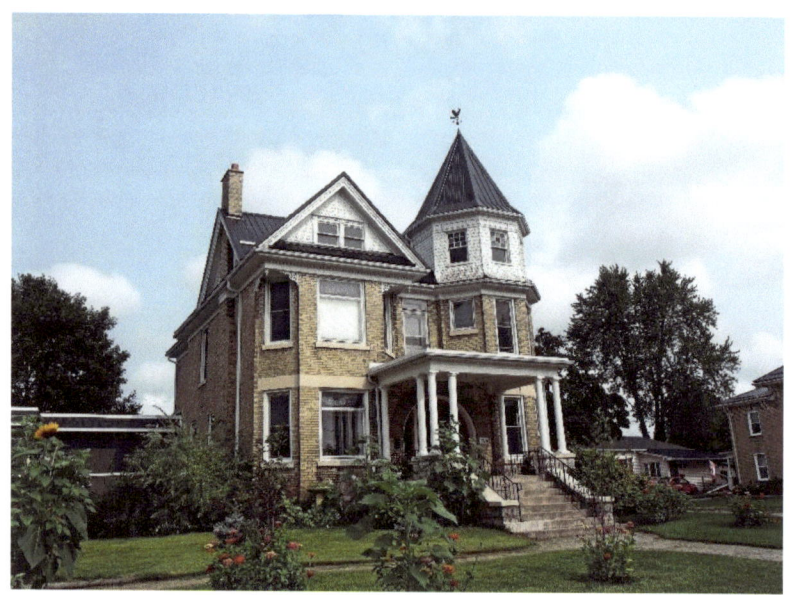
129 Albert Street - turret

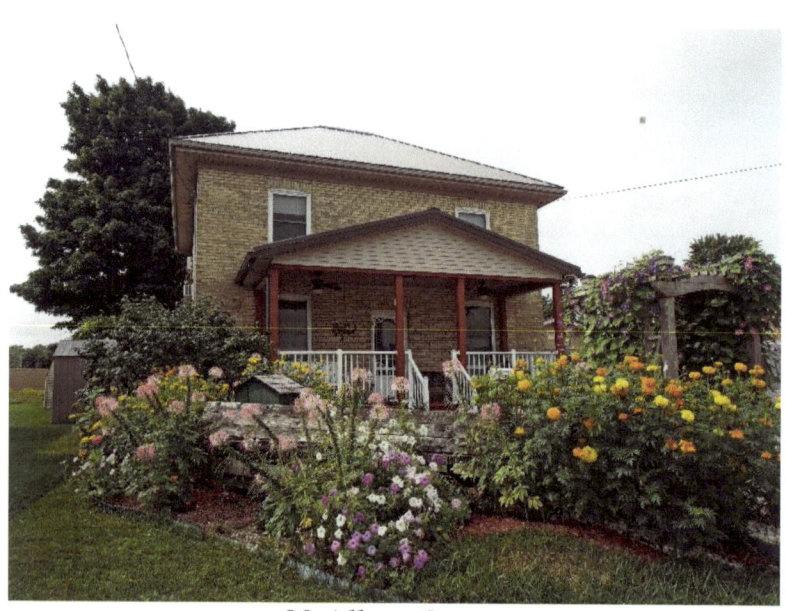
90 Albert Street

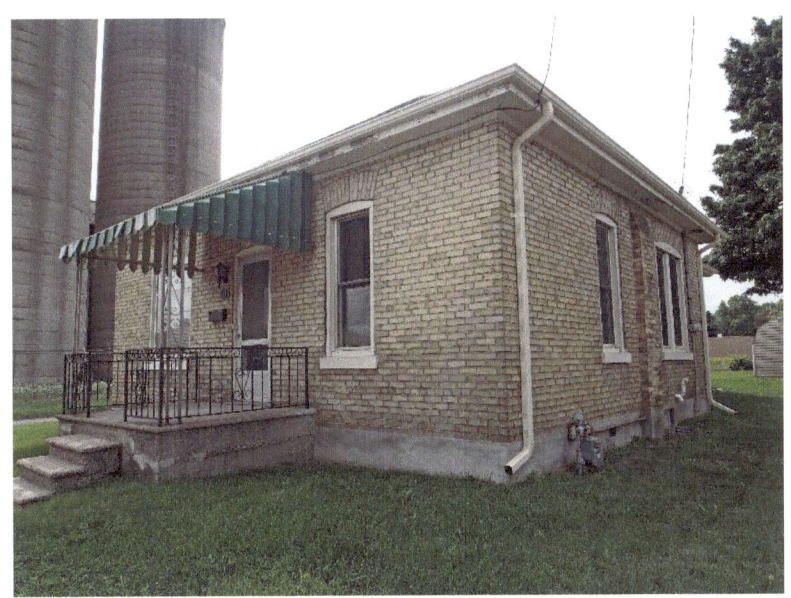

86 Albert Street

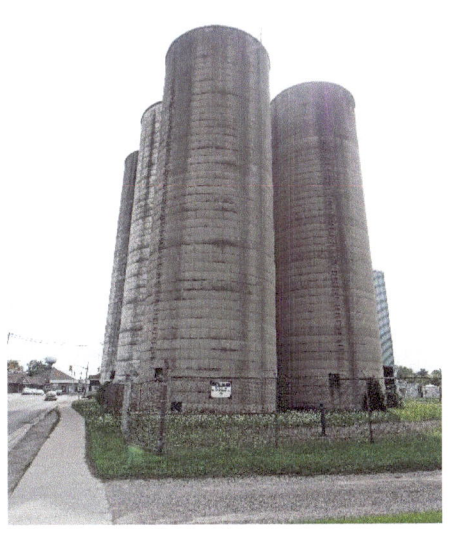

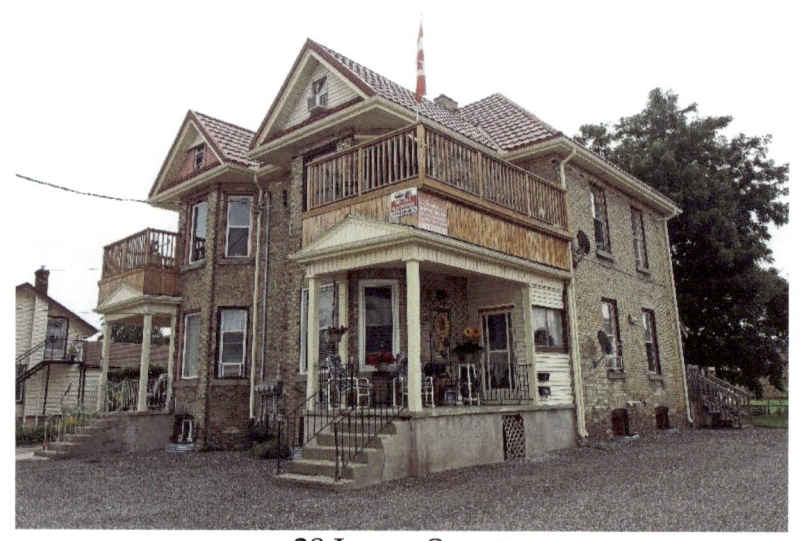

28 James Street

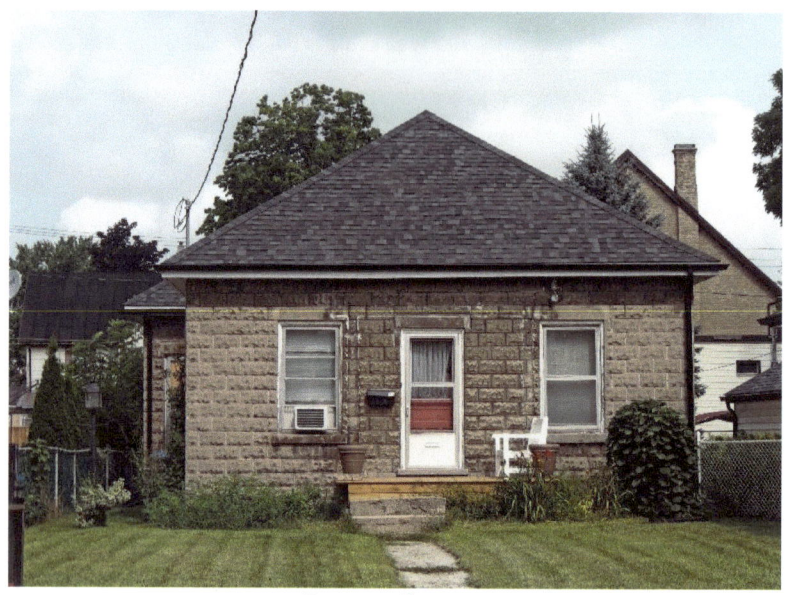

James Street

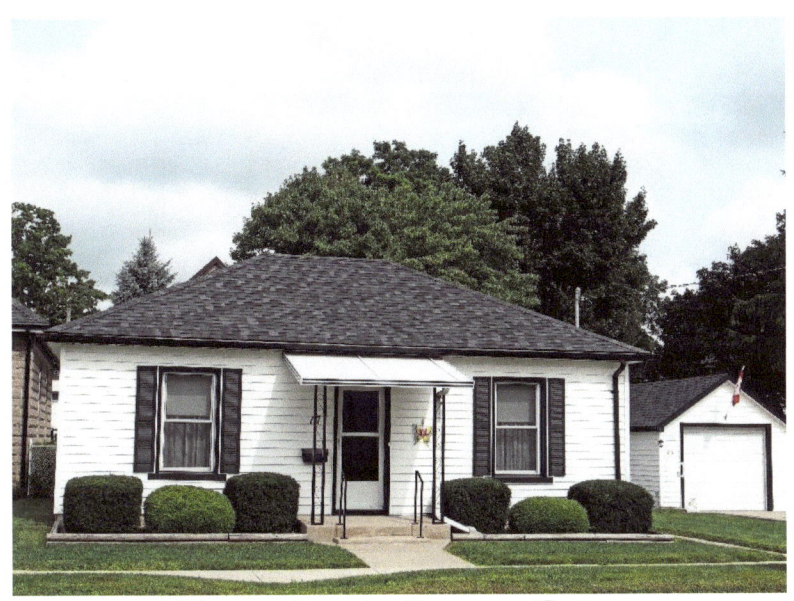

17 James Street – Regency Cottage

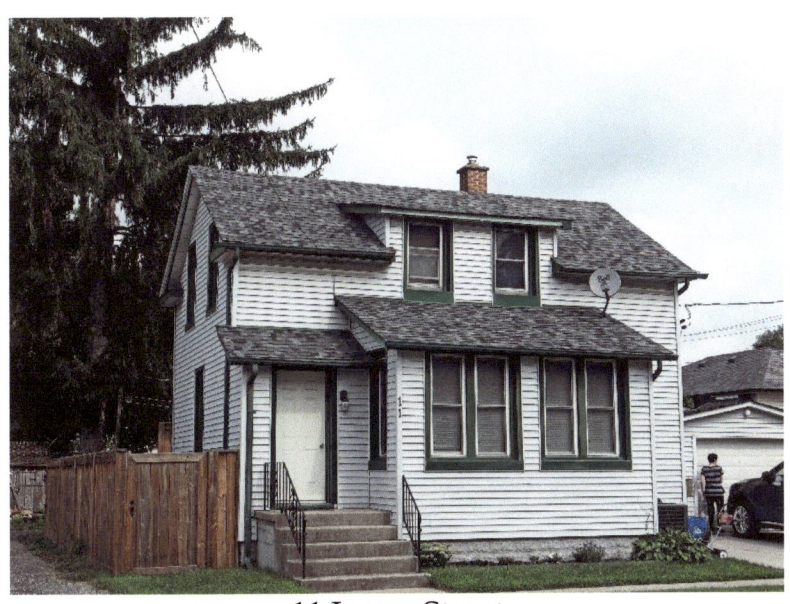

11 James Street

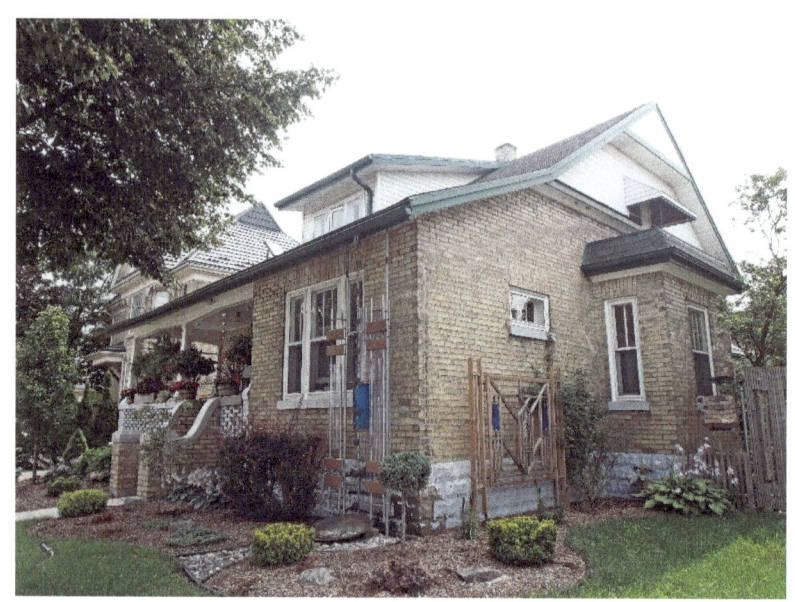
10 James Street

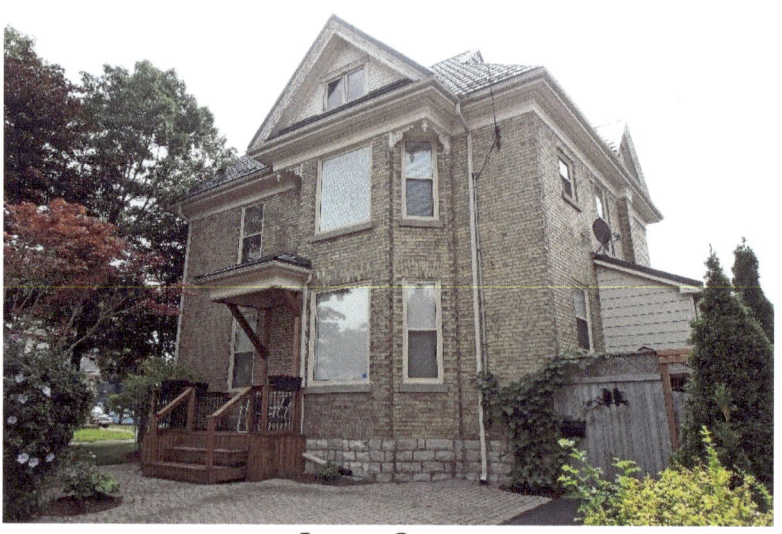
James Street

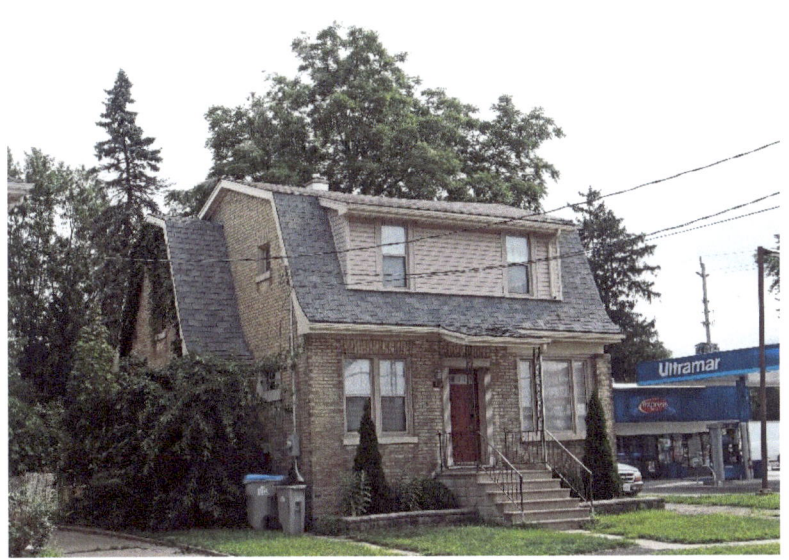

19 Caradoc Street – gambrel roof

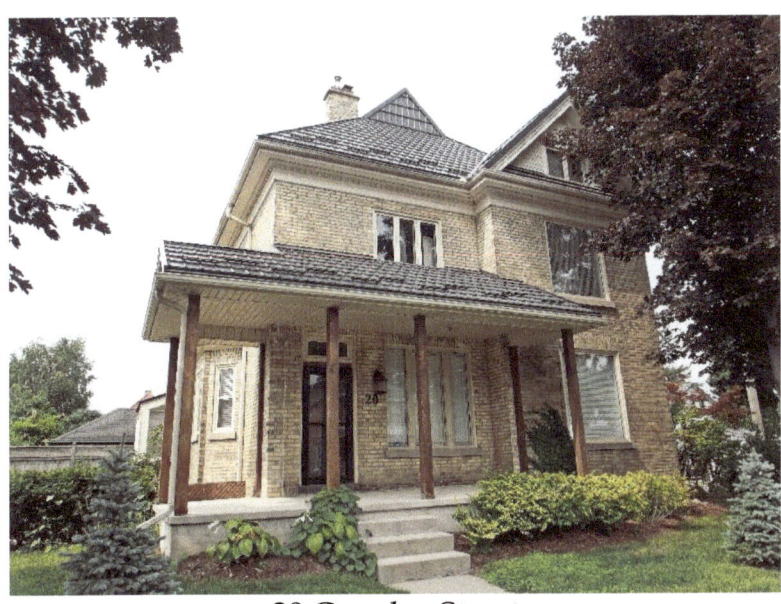

20 Caradoc Street

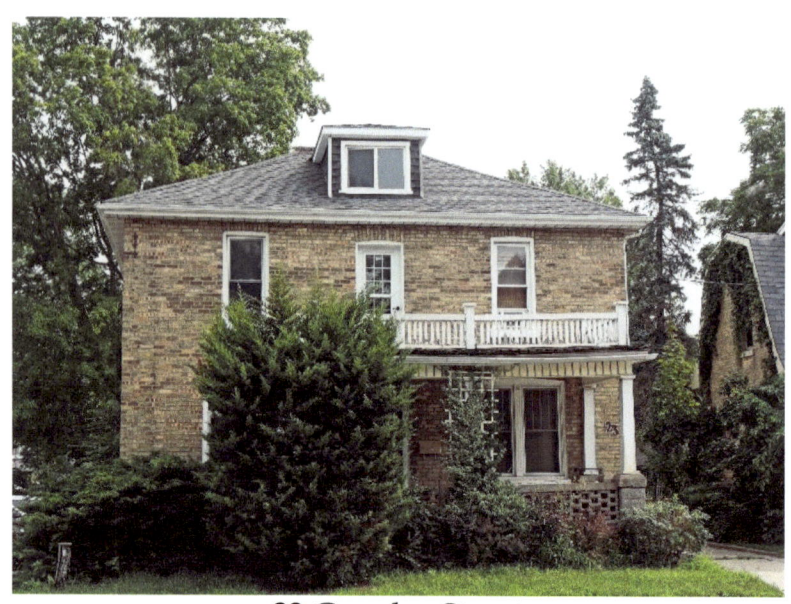

23 Caradoc Street

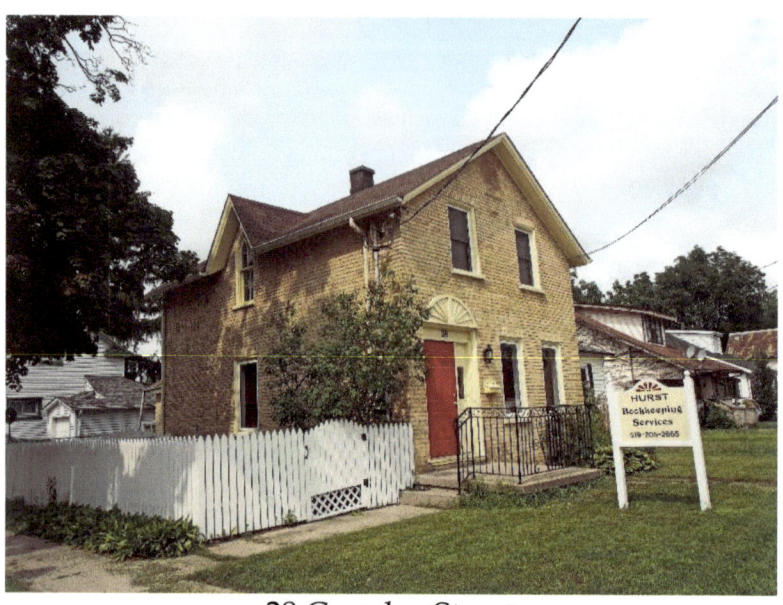

28 Caradoc Street

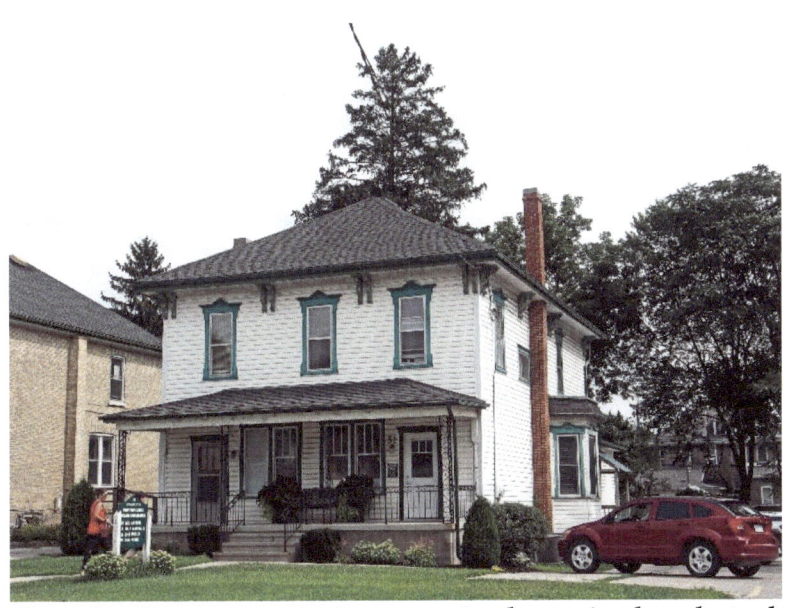

31 Caradoc Street – two-storey, paired cornice brackets, bay window on side

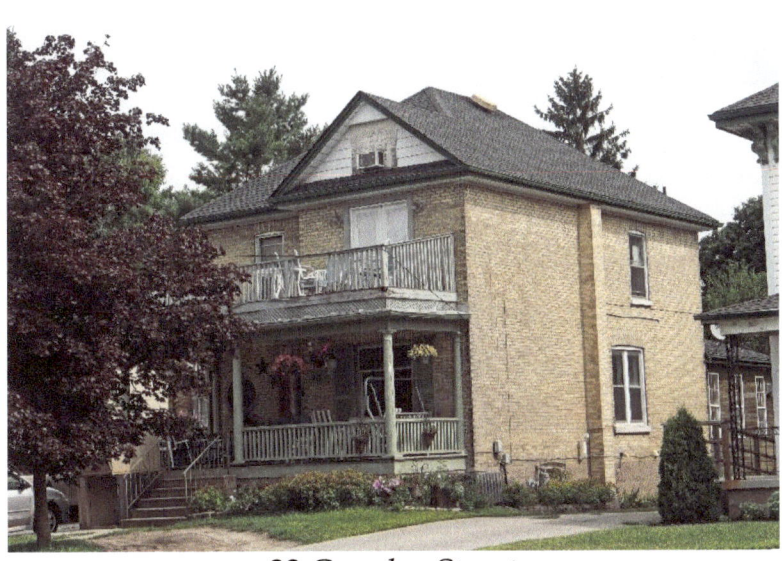

33 Caradoc Street

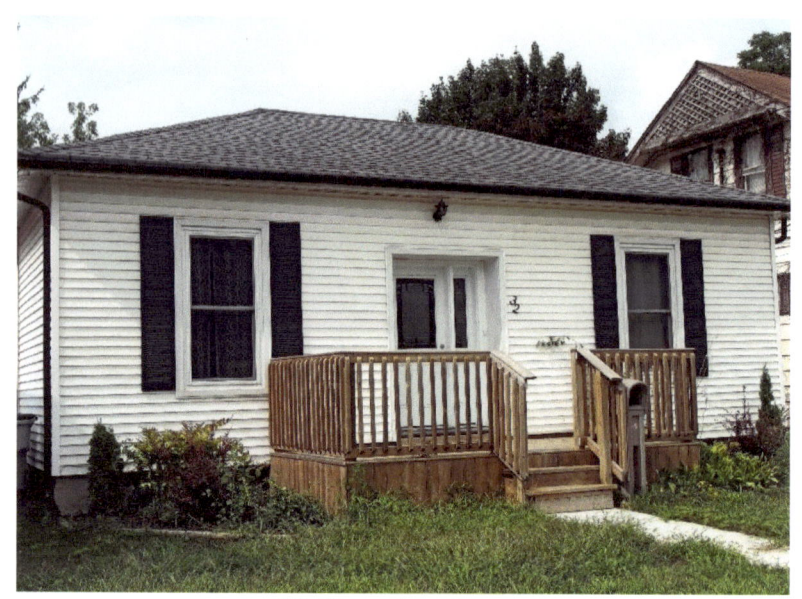

32 Caradoc Street

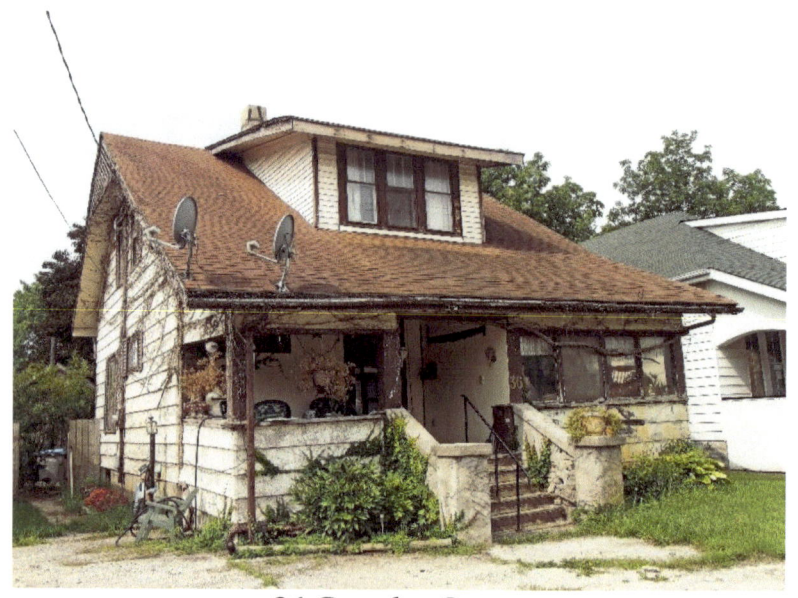

36 Caradoc Street

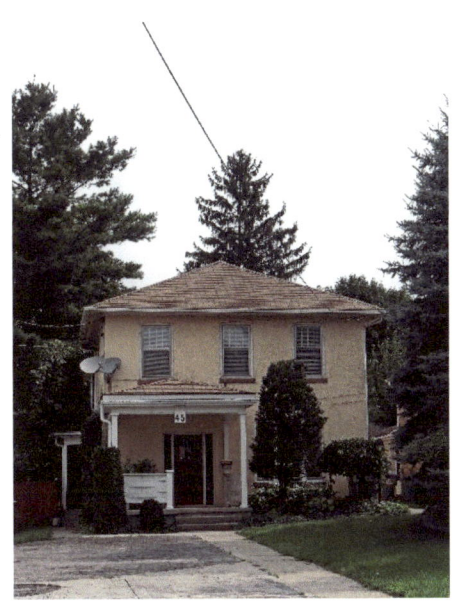

45 Caradoc Street

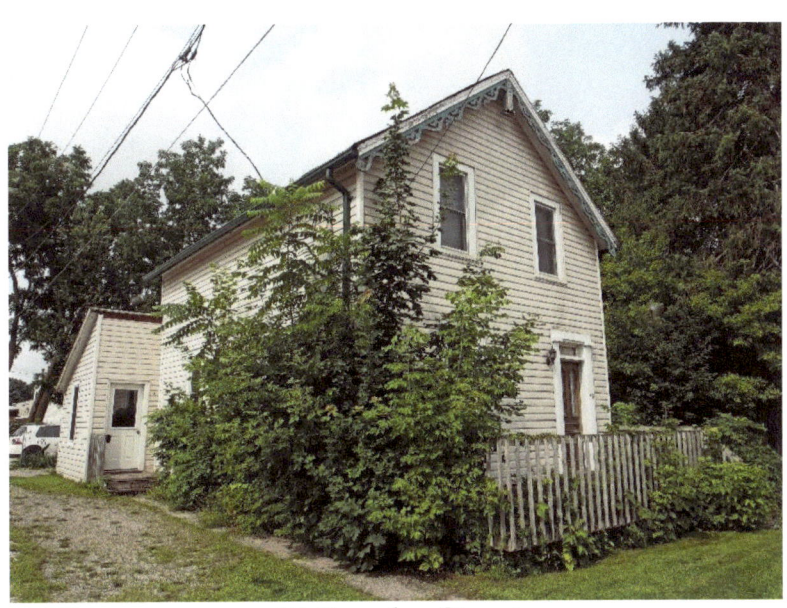

46 Caradoc Street

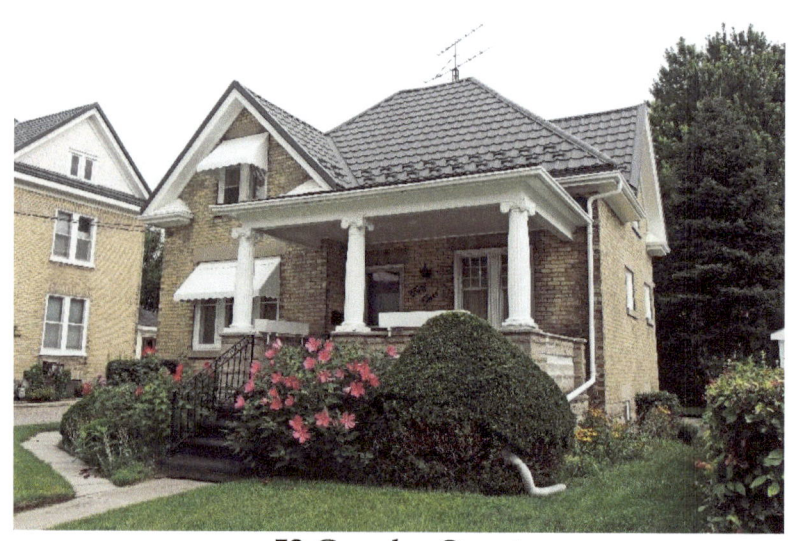

53 Caradoc Street

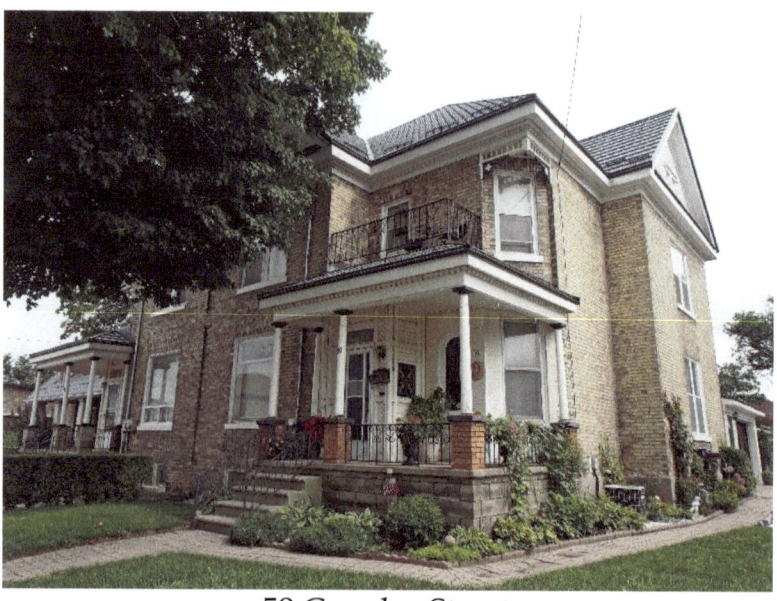

59 Caradoc Street

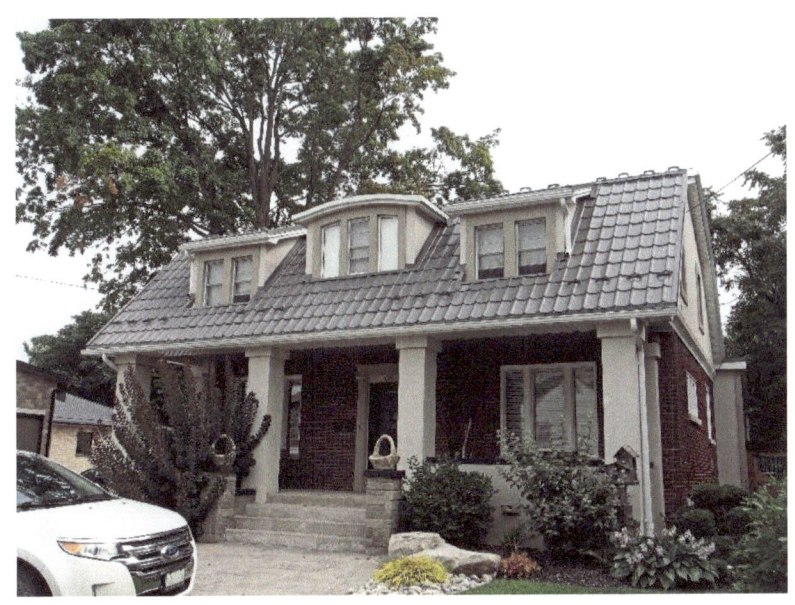

69 Caradoc Street – dormers in the gambrel roof

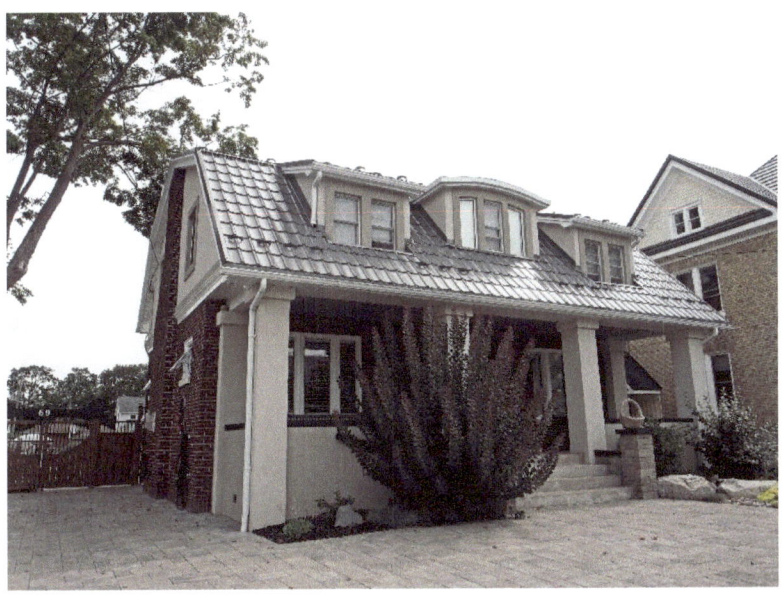

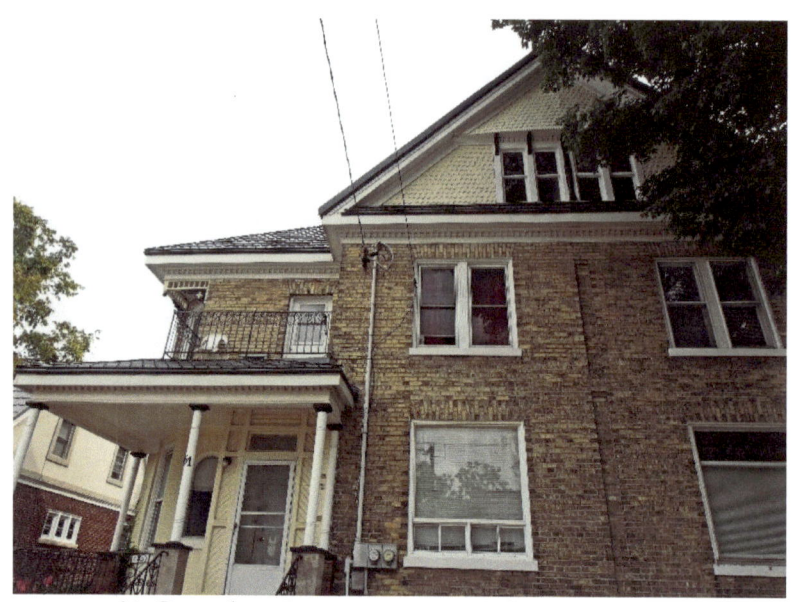

61 Caradoc Street – second floor balcony

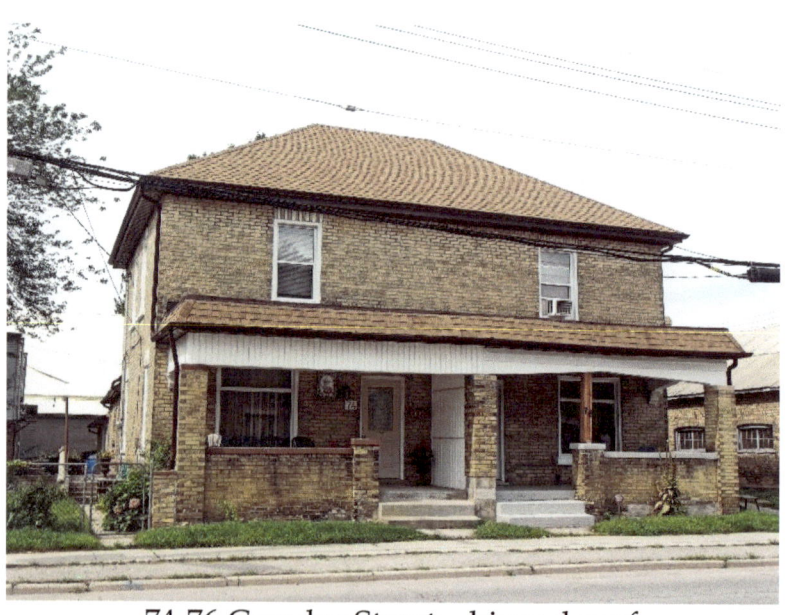

74-76 Caradoc Street – hipped roof

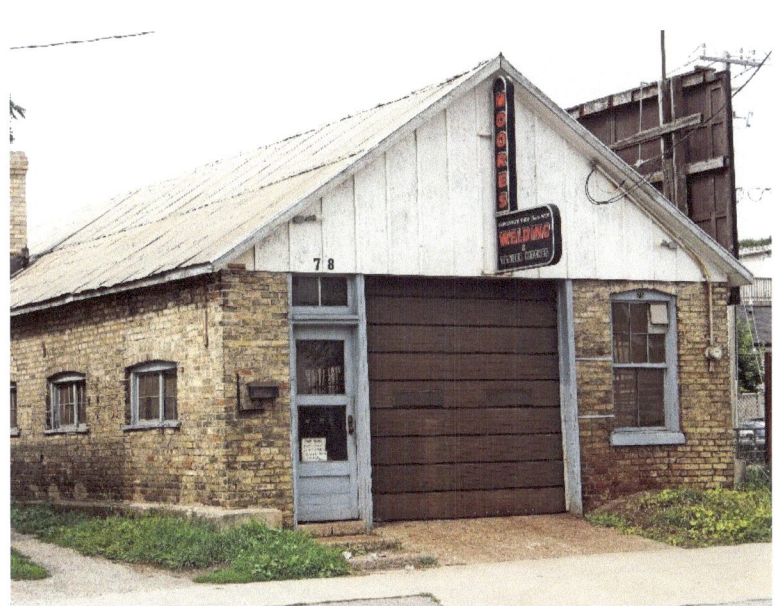

78 Caradoc Street – a blacksmith shop since the 1880s

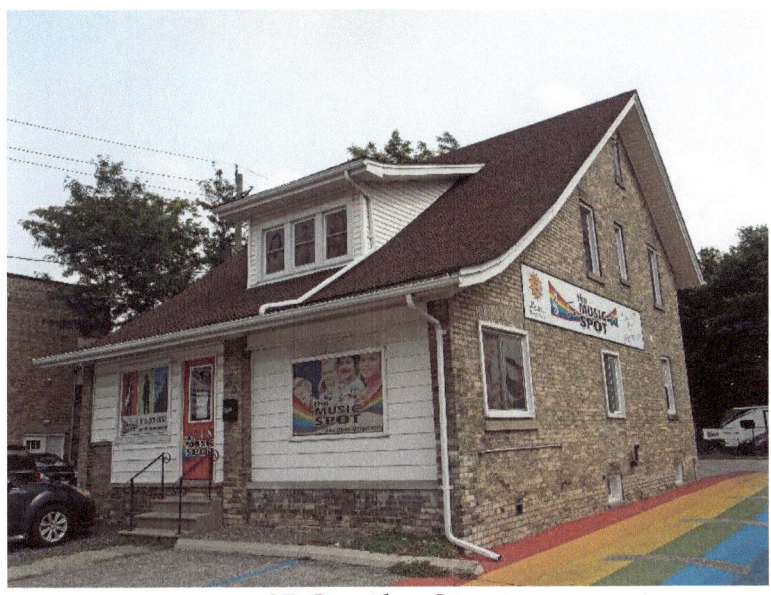

85 Caradoc Street

Other Books by Barbara Raue

Coins of Gold
Arrows, Indians and Love
The Life and Times of Barbara
The Cromwell Family Book
Laura Secord Discovered
Daddy Where Are You?

Montana Series
Book 1: Montana Dream
Book 2: Life on the Montana Frontier
Book 3: Montana to Boston and Back
Book 4: Montana Sons Go to War
Book 5: Montana Sons Return from War

© 2019 by Barbara Raue - All the photos in this book have been taken with my cameras. I own the rights to them.

www.ingramcontent.com/pod-product-compliance
Lightning Source LLC
Chambersburg PA
CBHW040238220526
45473CB00001B/286